# TOTAL TRANSITION

SANDEEP PAI AND
SAVANNAH CARR-WILSON

# TOTAL
# TRANSITION

*The Human Side of the
Renewable Energy Revolution*

**RMB**

RMB | Rocky Mountain Books Ltd.
rmbooks.com
@rmbooks
facebook.com/rmbooks

Cataloguing data available from Library and Archives Canada
ISBN 9781771602488 (paperback)
ISBN 9781771602495 (electronic)

All photographs are by the authors unless otherwise noted.

Design by Chyla Cardinal
Cover photo by Parwaz Ahmed Khan
Printed and bound in Canada by Friesens

Distributed in Canada by Heritage Group Distribution and in the U.S. by Publishers Group West

For information on purchasing bulk quantities of this book, or to obtain media excerpts or invite the author to speak at an event, please visit rmbooks.com and select the "Contact us" tab.

We acknowledge the financial support of the Government of Canada through the Canada Book Fund and the Canada Council for the Arts, and of the province of British Columbia through the British Columbia Arts Council and the Book Publishing Tax Credit.

Canada Council    Conseil des arts
for the Arts       du Canada

BRITISH COLUMBIA

BRITISH COLUMBIA ARTS COUNCIL
An agency of the Province of British Columbia

### Disclaimer

The views expressed in this book are those of the authors and do not necessarily reflect those of the publishing company, its staff or its affiliates.

*To our parents,*
*Catherine Carr,*
*Hersh Kline,*
*D.D. Ramanandan*
*and Geeta Ramanandan.*
*Thank you for everything.*

# CONTENTS

# ACKNOWLEDGEMENTS

We are deeply grateful to those who took the time to speak with us and share their knowledge and perspectives while we were researching this book, including (in order of appearance): Suresh Bhuiyan, Robert Grandjambe, Yahya Al-Abdullah, Professor Zoltán Illés, Giriraj Kumar, Arun Kumar Singh, Ramendra Kumar, Raju Munda, Ashok Agarwal, Santosh, Shankar Paswan, Urmila Devi, Parshooram Yadav, Mohan Bhuiyan, S.P. Singh, Ohmprakash Bhuiyan, Gopal Ji, Srikumari Devi, Titri Devi, Dananjee Sharma, Mangli Bhuiyan, Santosh Bhuiyan, Kundan Paswan, Jay Bueckert, Ken Smith, Peter, Harvey, Alvaro Pinto, Karla Buffalo, Terry Abel, Raymond Ladouceur, Melody Lepine, Robert Grandjambe Sr., Andrew Moore, Cedrick Todwell, Karen Basiye, Purnima Kumar, Nikhil Nair, Vaclav Smil, Chandra Bhushan and Lliam Hildebrand. In particular, we are grateful to Suresh Bhuiyan, Srikumari Devi and Robert Grandjambe for spending a great deal of time with us in order to share their experiences and stories.

The way our family, friends and community came together to support this project really moved and inspired us both. We are grateful to our parents – Catherine Carr, Hersh Kline, D.D. Ramanandan and Geeta Ramanandan – for their full support of this project, and for their creative ideas and careful editing as reviewers. We would also like to thank Sandeep's uncle, Sudhir Das, for believing in us and our project, and for helping us however he could from the very beginning.

Special thanks to Gośka Lekan for contributing her creative genius to help us get our Kickstarter off the ground, and to our classmates Dann Moreno, Marouko Tsagkari and Sunanda Mehta, who jumped in to contribute in the first hour of our Kickstarter campaign and helped it take off.

A very big thank you to Parwaz Ahmed Khan for helping tell the story of Jharia through his lens, to Georgia Lloyd-Smith for helping connect us to many of the thoughtful people we were fortunate to have a chance to speak to in Canada, and to Liz Drachenberg for always being ready to listen to new ideas, thoroughly review drafts with both a green and a yellow highlighter and help decide between hundreds of photos. A big thank you to Brayton Noll and Dasha Mihailova for listening to many of our preliminary ideas, contributing helpful insights in their review of early drafts and for always staying enthusiastic about and interested in our project. Finally, we would like to thank Erin Gray for her thoughtful edits, and Arun Subramaniam, our final reviewer, for challenging us to think deeply about this topic and to produce the best work possible.

We really appreciated the support of the MESPOM program, especially that of the following Central European University professors: Dr. Aleh Cherp, Dr. László Pintér and Dr. Zoltán Illés. We also appreciated Lund University professor Håkan Rodhe's enthusiastic help – both with our Kickstarter and during our semester in Sweden – and MESPOM alumni Karen Basiye, Purnima Kumar and Leo Akwany's assistance during our time in Kenya. Finally, a special thanks to Gyorgyi Puruczky – you really went above and beyond to help us make this project a success.

We would like to thank everyone who contributed to our Kickstarter crowdfunding campaign. We were blown away by your generosity, and you truly helped make this book a reality. We would also like to thank Mr. Nigel Press for believing in our creative idea and for generously supporting our project, and the Central European University Foundation, Budapest, for disbursing the Lydia Press Memorial Fund grants (the book represents our ideas but doesn't necessarily reflect the opinion of CEUBPF). We are also grateful to the staff of Massolit Café in Budapest, Hungary, for letting us film our Kickstarter video in the café's beautiful backyard.

Finally, we are grateful to each other for the strong 50-50 working partnership that we fostered throughout the book-writing process. It wasn't totally equal, though – Sandeep often consumed the entire contents of the fridge, while Savannah drank all the tea.

*Part I*

———

# A JOURNEY BEGINS

## Chapter One

# BEGINNINGS IN BUDAPEST

His eyes, set in a weathered face, were red from the coal dust blowing through the village. Standing next to his house, dressed in a skirt-like lungi and a dirty yellow and grey striped work shirt, he told us, "The coal industry is dirty, and I am dying a slow death living here. But I have no other option." A thin and wiry coal worker, Suresh Bhuiyan was vocal about his situation when we met him in Jharia – the heart of India's coal mining belt. "If I got the opportunity, I would love to work in the solar industry, but how will I find a job? My present is painful, but the future is uncertain."

On the other side of the world, 11,000 kilometres from Jharia, we met Robert Grandjambe – another fossil fuel industry worker. We first met Robert in Fort McMurray, Alberta, the hub of Canada's oil sands operations. A well-built man in his early 30s, Robert is a member of the Mikisew Cree First Nation. A fourth-generation trapper and hunter, he told us that he works as a millwright in the oil sands industry. "The oil sands has environmental impacts, but many people from my community are economically dependent on it for their livelihood. I would love to work in the renewable energy industry, be it solar or wind, but will I get work there? Who would help? Government? It's uncertain," he said.

Ten months earlier, when we started our master's degrees in Budapest, Hungary, we never thought we would travel to opposite ends of the world and meet Suresh and Robert, who would raise similar questions about their future in a world moving towards a renewable energy transition.

Our story began in September 2015. We had just arrived in Budapest – Savannah from British Columbia in western Canada, and Sandeep from Jharkhand in eastern India. We came to Hungary to start a two-year Erasmus Mundus Masters Course in Environmental Sciences, Policy, and Management (affectionately called MESPOM). The course would take us from Central European University (CEU) in Budapest, to the University of the Aegean in Greece and finally to Lund University in Sweden. Savannah had just finished an environmental law degree in Canada. Sandeep was taking a break after five years working as an investigative journalist in India for some of the country's leading English-language newspapers. We were both very excited to start our master's program at CEU, a diverse university with students from more than 130 countries.

As we each stepped through the automatic glass doors of the CEU Residence Center, our home for the first eight months of our master's, we didn't know we would meet, fall in love, write a book to address burning questions we shared about environmental issues and spend the coming summer in India and Canada, interviewing people from all walks of life.

We met in the first week of September, during our orientation week. The CEU Residence Center was far outside the city centre, about an hour from our university. We had to take a bus, then a metro, and then walk for 15 minutes to reach 609, our classroom on the sixth floor of the brick CEU building in downtown Budapest. This meant we had a lot of time to talk along the way. On a bright Wednesday morning, we were walking towards the bus station outside the Residence Center with a group of classmates when we hit it off talking about Indian food. "My whole family's vegetarian, and cooks a lot of Indian food," Savannah said. "We love it!"

Sandeep raised his eyebrows with a big smile. "I love cooking Indian food. Maybe someday soon I will cook for you and other classmates," he offered.

"Great – definitely!" Savannah said. And so our relationship began.

By October, we were dating, thanks to the spicy power of Indian food and our realization that we both enjoyed discussing the tough and thorny environmental issues facing the world. Classes were also picking up at school as two major world events shaped conversations inside and outside of the classroom. The United Nations Climate Change Conference was set to take place in Paris at the end of November, and some were heralding these talks as the last chance for the world to address climate change before there was no turning back. At the same time, the Syrian refugee crisis continued to make daily headlines both around the world and a few kilometres from our school, in Budapest's main train station. In September, the Hungarian prime minister, Viktor Orbán, built a wall to keep refugees out of the country. When the wall was finished, desperate refugees fleeing north towards Germany and other parts of Europe were forced to find other routes, with many travelling through neighbouring Croatia.

Both the Paris climate talks and the Syrian refugee crisis were big topics in our department that fall – the climate talks for obvious reasons, and the refugee crisis because of a growing global interest in a connection between it and climate change. In early September, Brandon Anthony, our Canadian professor, started off our Non-Human Biosphere course by placing climate change in context for us. He told us that new studies were emerging linking the refugee crisis to the changing climate in Syria. As conditions became drier in the Syrian countryside, internally displaced people moved to cities, where it was difficult for them to find jobs. Urban areas became conflict incubators.

One such study – by climate scientists from the University of California, Santa Barbara and Columbia University – argued that climate change was a significant factor that contributed to the severe 2007–10 Syrian drought.[1] Because of the drought, more than 1.5 million people migrated from rural farming areas to the peripheries of urban centres. "The rapidly growing urban peripheries of Syria, marked by illegal settlements, overcrowding, poor infrastructure, unemployment, and crime, were neglected by the Assad government and became the heart of the developing unrest," said the study. After that class, Sandeep talked to Yahya Al-Abdullah, a CEU student who comes from a farming family in southern Aleppo, Syria. Yahya emphasized Brandon's point. "In my city of Aleppo, suddenly, millions of people started settling down in illegal colonies in areas like Salah Aldien, Bani Zaid, and so on. They were farmers and migrants and were mainly affected by drought. These illegal colonies became the main centres of protest," he told Sandeep.[2]

One day in mid-October, after attending multiple morning classes in the warm 609 classroom, we decided to get some fresh air. We had a 50-minute lunch break between classes and set out to walk along the Danube. Europe's second-longest river, the wide, blue-grey Danube originates in Germany, runs through the heart of Budapest and terminates in the Black Sea. It divides Buda and Pest, the two ancient halves of the city. A walk along the riverbank on the Pest side, five minutes from CEU, offers stunning views of the ancient Buda castle.

"Ever since Brandon's class and talking to Yahya, I've really wanted to write an article about the refugee crisis and climate change," Sandeep said as we walked. "I want to keep up my journalism work during the master's, and I think a newspaper back home in India would be really interested."

"Sure, especially because the Paris climate change talks are about to happen," Savannah said. "Unless countries agree to do something significant and binding, I think we're going to start seeing a lot more displaced people... it's scary."

"Well, let me tell you something that will shock you," Sandeep said. "Most people in India don't care about climate change – they don't even know what it is."

"Really?" Savannah said with surprise. "But what about academics, or people in government?"

"Of course, some of them will know! But definitely not the common person on the street. They have absolutely no idea," Sandeep said. "My parents, my friends and family, they won't know what climate change is." He explained that in India, most people are more concerned about basic issues like hunger, poverty and unemployment. Millions of people have no access to electricity. Climate change matters, but it isn't at the top of the list. Sandeep paused, looking out at the Danube waterfront. "In India, it's a dilemma. To develop the country, India actually has to keep mining and burning fossil fuels like coal – but at the Paris talks, there's pressure to make commitments to move away from that, towards renewable energy sources like solar."

"That's so interesting," Savannah said, stopping to tie a flapping shoelace. "It's a big issue," she said as she got up. "Even in Canada, a big part of the economy in certain parts depends on the oil sands – but there's also pressure and some support to move towards renewables."

"The other thing that no one thinks about is jobs," Sandeep said. "It would be great for India to move towards 100 per cent renewable energy – but what about the millions of people employed in the coal mines? I've seen it myself in my journalism work. Coal mining employs *hundreds of thousands* of people in India directly, and several *millions* more are indirectly dependent on the survival of this industry."

"True," said Savannah, "we need to move away from fossil fuels, but we also have to think about these other really critical connected issues." She paused and looked around. "But hey, we've almost done a circle here, and we're close to CEU. I think we'd better head back to class, or we'll miss the first chunk of the lecture."

Our conversation that day planted a seed in our minds. We kept thinking about it over the course of the next month. In mid-November, the two of us went on a trip to Kraków, Poland. Our Polish classmate, Malgorzata Lekan (who preferred to be called Gośka), gave us some recommendations of what not to miss. She knew we were foodies and insisted we visit a *bar mleczny*, or milk bar. Milk bars are a type of cafeteria-style restaurant with a menu based on dairy products. They were popular during the communist period and known for providing good nutrition to Polish people through traditional food and milk products – including the famous Polish pierogi.

Walking down a cobblestone lane in the centre of Kraków, Savannah grabbed Sandeep's arm. "There's one!" she said, pointing.

For the last hour, Sandeep had been talking about how hungry he was. "Let's go and attack!" he said with a laugh.

Inside Milkbar Tomasza, we gratefully shed our layers in the steamy indoor heat. A few minutes later, we sat down to hot plates of pierogi generously topped with sour cream and chives.

After five minutes of complete silence and ten pierogi, Sandeep said, "I've been thinking about something, and I have a crazy idea. Do you want to hear it?" Savannah nodded as she stuffed a loaded bite of pierogi and sour cream into her mouth. "It's about our summer." We had a two-month break between the end of our second semester in Greece and the beginning of our third semester in Sweden. "I know you've been thinking about looking for an internship," he said. "But I have a different idea. Think of it as a Plan B."

"Just tell me the idea, I want to know!" Savannah said, spearing another pierogi.

"What if – just what if – we write a book this summer," Sandeep said. Savannah's eyes widened. He put both palms on the table and leaned forward. "I'm still thinking about that job question – what will happen to the millions of people in the world who are dependent on the fossil fuel industry if we transition to renewable energy? How are they currently living, and what challenges are they facing? Is anyone thinking about it? How will the world transition, and at what speed? I think we should explore that this summer, and do it by meeting and talking to the people who are at the front lines of this transition."

"Uh... a book!" Savannah said. She ate a few more pierogi and chewed thoughtfully, while Sandeep stared at her hopefully. "I like it. I like the idea," she said, after a moment of silence. "And I don't think it should be Plan B. I think this is what we should do, period."

Sandeep started to look excited. "And just think," he said. "We've been talking about these issues for months, in class and outside of class, on our own. But if we write this book, we'll have a chance to actually speak to some of the real people who are affected by these issues and tell their stories. That's what I'm interested in. Not just some random theories, but what's happening on the ground."

For the rest of the meal, we kept talking about it. We agreed it was a great idea, but we also knew that doing field research for a book like this would take a lot of money – money that we didn't have for the summer. We agreed to keep thinking about it.

After we returned to Budapest and classes started up again, the idea kept floating around in the back of our heads, but we didn't have time to work on it. When Christmas break came, Savannah went home to Canada to spend the holidays with her family, and Sandeep stayed in Budapest at the Residence Center with nothing but time on his hands. Partway through her vacation, Savannah got an email from Sandeep. "I wrote a book proposal," he said in the email. *What?!* Savannah thought to herself.

We spoke via Skype a few days later. "The book proposal looks great," Savannah said, "but are we really serious about this? And how can we get the funding to do it?"

"Well," Sandeep said, "let's decide if we want to do it first, then let's figure out how." He laughed. "Did I ever tell you about this verb in Hindi, *jugad*?" Savannah shook her head. "It means to manage it, somehow. We'll find a way – or if we can't find a way, we'll make one! That's what we're going to do – *jugad* it!" We both laughed.

After a few more calls, we decided we were serious. We wanted to investigate our burning questions, and we didn't want to do it solely from classroom 609 in Budapest. We wanted to speak to real people who were being affected by the big ideas that high-ranking diplomats were talking about and making decisions about at the Paris climate talks.

Once we made up our minds to write this book, things started to fall in place. We fixed up the book proposal. We decided to do two case studies to investigate our questions: one in Alberta, Canada, home of the oil sands and the site of a serious decline in fossil-fuel-related jobs in recent years, and one in Jharia, Jharkhand – a town in India that's been on fire for 100 years due to unscientific coal mining. We also wanted to explore hopeful initiatives in the growing world of renewable energy and hoped to do that in India and Canada, as well as throughout the rest of our master's degrees. We showed the proposal to two professors we trusted, who gave us invaluable advice and suggested an initial funding source – the Lydia Press Memorial Fund.

The father of a late MESPOM student, Lydia Press, set up this bursary to fund thesis-related field research in developing countries – the type of research Lydia was passionate about before she died in a tragic mountaineering accident in the French Alps during her MESPOM degree. This was our first challenge. Could we convince Nigel Press to fund our field research, even though it wasn't linked to our master's theses and no one had done anything like this before? We sent the proposal to Nigel but heard nothing for two weeks. Deciding we had nothing to lose, we made a nervous phone call to Nigel one evening through a bad Skype connection, sitting on the ground floor of the CEU building.

"Hello Mr. Press?" Sandeep said. "Sandeep here. I had sent you a funding proposal about my book a few weeks ago through email. Have you – have you seen it?" Nigel told Sandeep that he had seen it, and asked him a few more questions. *Time for jugad!* Sandeep thought, and he began to explain the book with great excitement.

They spoke for a few more minutes. "I'll get back to you soon," Nigel told Sandeep. After Sandeep hung up, we looked at each other. The future of our project hung on our ability to get some initial funding to pay for our field research costs – and this was our best lead so far. Without Nigel's grant, our project might drown in the Danube.

A few days later, we were sitting in the CEU Residence Center computer lab, working on an assignment. The computer lab, a small room full of anxious master's students churning out work close to their deadlines, smelled strongly of sweat, stale coffee and printer ink. Taking a break from the rather boring assignment, Savannah checked her email. Turning to Sandeep, she said, "Hey – HEY! I've got an email from Nigel! And he's decided to give me a grant!"

"Wait, let me check too," said Sandeep. "I got one too!" We got up from the computers, went into the hallway and danced in happiness.

"It's the beginning! It's happening!" said Savannah.

It wasn't a straight or easy road from there. We tried ten or more funding sources but had no success. After a month passed, we spoke with one of our professors and mentors, Dr. László Pintér. At first, he couldn't think of any other funding sources we hadn't already tried. Then, after a pause in the conversation, he said, "Have you considered crowdfunding?" We hadn't, and we weren't sure about it. Crowdfund our research? How did you even start a crowdfunding campaign?

Eventually, we decided to do it, and as with everything we take on, we threw our all into it. We decided that if we were going to *jugad* our research, we had to try everything. We did a self-guided crash course in crowdfunding. After creating a Kickstarter website, we enlisted the help of our Polish classmate, Gośka. She happened to be really talented with a camera – in addition to having great pierogi recommendations – and helped us make our crowdfunding video. We came up with creative "no packaging, no shipping" rewards to offer those who donated, as we wanted to run the most environmentally friendly Kickstarter possible. In the first eight days, we met our funding goal of C$3,500 (about US$2,600), and then surpassed it, reaching 140 per cent of our goal by the end of our 30-day campaign. More than 100 backers from all over the world, both friends and strangers, supported our idea. This, along with the Lydia Press bursaries, was enough for us to cover our basic research costs, although we also kicked in some of our personal funds for two plane tickets we couldn't otherwise cover.

Sandeep spent a month navigating the Canadian immigration system and, with the help of professors and administrators in the MESPOM program who gave letters of support, got a visa to go to Canada. Soon afterwards, Savannah applied for and received a visa for India. We started to build up contacts in both places and lock down the details. Doing all this was not easy amidst a busy master's program. We managed with a lot of help from our professors and classmates, and coffee. Our passion for the topic kept us going, and by May 2016, we had come a long way from a plate of pierogi in Poland.

During our semester, while working to make this book a reality, we also spent a lot of time deepening our knowledge. We spent hours discussing each other's country's context for energy transition. We read about the world's dependence on fossil fuels, climate change, the environmental impacts of fossil fuel extraction and use, the history of energy transitions and global progress towards renewable energy. We discussed these topics with each other, with friends and with family. On Fridays, our MESPOM friends would joke, "Are you guys researching the book again this weekend?"

During this time, we had the chance to talk the topic over for the first time with someone beyond our inner circle – our professor Dr. Zoltán Illés, ardent environmentalist and former Hungarian state secretary of environmental protection, nature conservation and water management. He is a well-known and controversial Hungarian politician and an enthusiastic and opinionated professor, so we were excited to hear what he thought of the world's prospects for transition towards renewables and its impact on people.

## Chapter Two

---

# HOOKED ON
# FOSSIL FUELS

*Time is running out, and the world will have to think about what
will happen to these people if a transition to renewables comes.*
—Zoltán Illés, former Hungarian state
secretary of environmental protection, nature
conservation and water management

When we arrived at the Central European University (CEU)
tenth-floor cafeteria to meet Professor Zoltán Illés for lunch,
we spotted him sitting across from someone in the middle of
the cafeteria's narrow hallway. Wearing a full black suit, hair
slicked back on his head and rimless glasses perched on his
nose, Zoltán sat next to a large stack of books and papers. He
spotted us at the end of the hallway. "I'll be free soon, just take
a seat," he said.

We were excited yet nervous, as this was one of the first
times we were going to pitch our book idea to someone important. In addition to being one of our professors in CEU's
Department of Environmental Sciences and Policy, Zoltán was
also a well-known Hungarian politician who had held the position of state secretary of environmental protection, nature
conservation and water management until 2014. Zoltán had
taught us in the first semester. We knew him more than he
knew us, and we certainly hadn't told him the details of our
book idea.

We sat down at the table behind him. The cafeteria was
noisy, packed with students and professors enjoying the day's
990-forint set menu (about US$3.60). The cafeteria was the

most popular place to eat on campus, chiefly because it served a two-course meal with soup and a big plate of food for a good price, and because it was located in a bright, sunny hall. Apart from both of us feeling nervous, Sandeep was starving, as always! However, we wanted to wait for Zoltán.

Thankfully, we didn't have to wait for more than five minutes. Zoltán stood up and enthusiastically shook the hand of the man he had been having lunch with. "*Viszlát* – bye!" he said. Turning around, he greeted us.

"Professor, have you already eaten?" Savannah said. "We were going to order but thought we'd wait for you."

"I've been here for about an hour, but I only ate some cake," he said, laughing. "Cake before lunch – that's how I like to eat! But I'll order with you now." Sandeep and I had already scanned the daily menu. Savannah ordered pumpkin soup and tomato-and-chickpea stew with couscous. Sandeep and Zoltán ordered bowls of the famous Hungarian goulash – neither a soup nor a stew, but something in between. Once the waitress left with our orders, Zoltán came straight to the point. "So you want to talk about a book!" he said. "Tell me more."

"We wanted you to be one of the first people to hear about it, because we really respect your opinion and would like to know what you think of our idea," Sandeep said, leaning forward enthusiastically. "Essentially, we want to write a book about the world's transition away from fossil fuel dependency towards renewable energy, and what this will mean for the millions of people in the world who depend on fossil fuel for their livelihoods."

"In other words, we want to talk about how the world needs to move quickly towards renewable energy to save the climate – and needs to think about making a smooth transition from the old as it moves to the new," Savannah added. "We want to explore these topics through people's stories, and plan on travelling to communities built up around fossil fuel extraction to interview the people who live and work there."

"Wow," Zoltán said, raising his eyebrows and pursing his

lips. "What an interesting topic. I've never heard of anyone taking this angle before." He paused and became silent for a moment, lost in thought, tapping his fingers on the table. We took this opportunity to take a few bites. "Everyone wants a transition," he said, "but no one thinks about the people involved. And you know, some private companies in Hungary are already moving in this direction."

"Really?" asked Savannah.

"Mátrai Erőmű, a big lignite-fired power plant – that's brown coal – has already seen the writing on the wall. They're owned by RWE, a German energy company. Although they're producing huge amounts of electricity from lignite, they've recently started building solar panels. They're the biggest electricity plant in Hungary, but thanks god, they know a transition is coming. They're trying to get ahead of the curve." Zoltán grinned. "But I don't think the government in Hungary or anyone else has any plan to help workers in the fossil fuel industry transition to renewable energy jobs."

"Right now," he continued, "Hungary is heavily dependent on fossil fuels. And Prime Minister Viktor Orbán isn't interested in renewables. In fact, he abolished the environment ministry after my time as environment minister." Zoltán is seen in Hungary as critically opposed to the prime minister's environmental policies. "But Viktor Orbán can't ignore climate change forever. Time is running out, and the world will have to think about what will happen to these people if a transition to renewables comes."

◆

That day, on our way home from university to the Residence Center, we started thinking more about fossil-fuel-based energy and our own dependency on it. Every day, to get to CEU, we had to commute about an hour from our door to classroom 609. We took the elevator from the sixth floor in the dorm to the ground floor, relying on electricity to run the elevator that carried us down. Then we walked to a bus stop across the road from our dorm and took a diesel-powered bus to the metro station. The metro, which runs on electricity, took 20 minutes to take us to the centre of town. From there, we walked the rest of the way to the university, took another elevator to our classroom on the sixth floor, started the electric kettle in our department's kitchen to make some tea before class, and inevitably got to class a few minutes late. When we finally arrived, clutching mugs of tea, we sat down in a classroom that was heated primarily by natural gas. Overall, approximately 73 per cent of the energy consumed in Hungary comes from fossil fuel sources like coal, oil and natural gas.[3] As we sat in the metro that day, travelling at high speed from the central station of Deák Ferenc tér out into the boonies, where our dorm was located, it really hit us that fossil-fuel-based energy was imprinted on every experience and taken for granted every minute of our daily lives.

One of the first questions we wrapped our minds around when we decided to write this book was: What is energy, really? We thought about this question, asked our friends and family members and read about it. Many diverse answers came out of these discussions. Some said they weren't so sure. For some, energy meant electricity. For others, energy meant what you use to move your car. And, for a few, it meant how well you feel every day – which is personal energy, not what we were asking about. Before you read the next paragraph, take a minute (and maybe a sip of coffee or tea), and try coming up with your own definition of energy.

It seems that energy is not an easily definable concept. The common definition of energy is "the capacity for doing work." But what does this mean? The term has been used since the 19th century to refer to a number of natural and human-generated phenomena. There are many different types of energy that we need in our everyday lives. According to prominent energy expert Vaclav Smil, the most common types are "heat (thermal energy), motion (kinetic or mechanical energy), light (electromagnetic energy), and the chemical energy of fuel and foodstuffs." For example, humans convert fossil fuels such as coal, oil and gas, which contain chemical energy, to thermal energy for purposes like cooking and heating.[4]

*Merriam-Webster's Dictionary* defines the term "fossil fuel" as a type of fuel that is formed under the surface of the earth and made up of plant and animal remains. At some point during our early schooling, we had both been forced to memorize the fact that fossil fuels are made up of hydrogen, carbon, oxygen, nitrogen and varying amounts of sulphur. Back then, sitting in chemistry class, we never could have imagined that we would one day write a book about fossil fuels.

Leaving aside these scientific terms, energy is essentially what we need to live our lives every day – for example, burning oil products to move our cars, using gas to cook on our stoves and using electricity to light our homes. It's clear that we need lots of energy every day. Yet, despite all the excitement about the growth of renewable energy, many people would be surprised to learn how much energy still comes from fossil fuels.

From Hungary, where we discovered that 73 per cent of energy comes from fossil fuels, we zoomed out to the rest of the world. We learned that fossil fuels are responsible for about 86 per cent of global energy consumption. Of that, oil makes up approximately 33 per cent, coal 29 per cent and natural gas 24 per cent. Today, renewable energy sources such as solar, wind and biomass contribute only 3 per cent, but they are growing fast. Hydropower adds roughly another 7 per cent, while nuclear makes up the remaining 4 per cent.[5]

We started to talk to a lot of our classmates about this topic, many of whom came from the world's two biggest economies. Four friends came from the United States, and three came from China. It became clear that the United States and China, as well as our home countries of India and Canada, were really dependent on fossil fuels.

In the United States, about 81 per cent of energy consumption comes from fossil fuel sources, and 10 per cent comes from renewables.[6] Most energy in the United States is used for electricity, transportation and industrial purposes – for example, by Americans who use electricity in their homes, drive cars and consume manufactured goods. The fossil fuel industry also employs at least 2.1 million people in the United States – more than double the population of countries like Bhutan. More than a million people work in the traditional coal, oil and gas sectors, and close to a million work in the retail trade, for example at gas stations.[7] Of course, these jobs often have a multiplier effect, generating other jobs in industries such as food services. This makes it especially hard to fully estimate the number of jobs linked to fossil fuels. China is even more dependent on fossil fuel for its energy consumption. About 88 per cent of its energy comes from fossil fuel sources, with about two-thirds of that coming from coal.[8] The coal industry is also a big employer in the country, employing more than six million people.[9]

When we looked at our own countries, we saw a similar picture. In India, Sandeep's home country, about 93 per cent of primary energy consumed comes from fossil fuel sources.[10] Coal is India's primary energy source and it accounts for a little less than two-thirds of energy consumption.[11] Overall, the Government of India's public-sector company Coal India Limited employs approximately 500,000 workers, both regular and contract.[12] Canada, where Savannah comes from, is relatively less dependent on fossil fuel for its energy consumption. In 2015, about 64 per cent of primary energy consumed came from coal, oil and natural gas, and roughly 26 per cent came from hydro.[13] However, the fossil fuel industry, and in particular the oil and gas industry, provides jobs. The Canadian Association of Petroleum Producers states that direct and indirect jobs taken together amount to more than 425,000 jobs in Canada.[14]

We were surprised to learn how much of global energy consumption still depended on fossil fuels. As we attended more lectures at CEU and read more about the harmful impact of burning fossil fuels to generate energy, we started to feel worried – and more motivated than ever to write this book.

Fossil fuel extraction, transportation and combustion have many serious environmental impacts. To give just a few examples, coal mining devastates landscapes, and burning coal pollutes the air. A collaborative study by Chinese and American researchers found that air pollution from burning coal caused 366,000 deaths in 2013 in China alone – wiping out a population equal to that of the metropolitan area of Victoria, Savannah's home town.[15] When it comes to oil, a highly visible impact is oil spills during production and transportation. In 1989, the tanker *Exxon Valdez* struck a reef in Prince William Sound, Alaska, spilling 42 million litres of crude oil, contaminating almost 2000 kilometres of shoreline and killing approximately 2,000 sea otters, 300 harbour seals and 250,000 seabirds.[16] Other, longer-term effects on the ecosystem persisted for years, and impacts linger even today. In April 2010, the BP *Deepwater Horizon* drill rig exploded in the Gulf of Mexico, leaking an estimated 650 million litres of crude oil into the gulf over 87 days until attempts to cap the well succeeded.[17] These are just a few examples. However, one of the impacts that the world is most worried about is global warming, a symptom of climate change, which humans are causing primarily by burning fossil fuels.

To understand how burning fossil fuels is warming our planet, it's important to first understand that Earth is surrounded by a type of greenhouse – a layer of gases (known as greenhouse gases) found in the atmosphere that acts as a thermal blanket keeping Earth warm. These gases are primarily water vapour, with smaller amounts of carbon dioxide ($CO_2$), methane and nitrous oxide. When the sun's rays pass through the atmosphere and warm Earth's surface, this heat is eventually radiated back towards space as infrared heat. However, it can't fully leave. The greenhouse gas molecules in the atmosphere reabsorb much of this heat and radiate it back towards Earth's surface, ensuring a warm, liveable temperature. This is a natural phenomenon. Unfortunately, human activity has been changing this natural phenomenon for the worse. For example, when humans burn fossil fuel – like when gasoline is burnt to power a car – the burning process combines carbon (from the fuel) with oxygen (from the air) to create $CO_2$. When this $CO_2$ enters the atmosphere, it amplifies the greenhouse effect – trapping more heat and warming Earth further.[18]

Imagine that Earth already has a blanket that keeps it at a perfect temperature, but that human beings have started adding extra blankets – and things are starting to really heat up. In the last 150 years, humans have raised atmospheric $CO_2$ levels from 280 parts per million (ppm) to 400 ppm. Burning fossil fuels is the most significant cause.[19] In 1988, the United Nations Environment Programme and the World Meteorological Organization established the Intergovernmental Panel on Climate Change (IPCC) to provide a clear scientific view on the current state of climate change and its impacts. In its *Fifth Assessment Report*, the IPCC states, "Emissions of $CO_2$ from fossil fuel combustion and industrial processes contributed about 78% of the total GHG [greenhouse gas] emissions increase from 1970 to 2010, with a similar percentage contribution for the increase during the period 2000 to 2010."[20] Burning fossil fuels also emits other harmful greenhouse gases, like methane. Other human activities, like land use change from clearing land for agriculture, also contribute smaller, but still significant, amounts of greenhouse gases, including $CO_2$, but the bottom line is that burning fossil fuels is the main culprit warming our Earth.[21]

Some people might think, especially if they are from a cold region of the world, that temperatures a few degrees warmer wouldn't be the worst thing. However, the implications of global climate change are very serious and will affect everyone on the planet. The more scientists study and attempt to understand the implications of climate change, the clearer it becomes that Earth is very temperature-sensitive. World temperature rose 0.85 degrees over the period 1880–2012 – and we are already seeing impacts like accelerated global sea level rise, increases in large-scale forest fires in areas such as the western United States, increases in heavy precipitation events, and more intense, prolonged droughts in some areas.[22]

Scientists concluded, and world leaders accepted at the 2009 Copenhagen Climate Change Conference, that any temperature increase beyond two degrees Celsius would be dangerous. In 2015, to great surprise, policymakers at the Paris climate talks decided to lower the target further to 1.5 degrees Celsius – a more ambitious goal that the world is likely to miss.[23] Dr. Ben Sanderson of the National Center for Atmospheric Research in Boulder, Colorado, told *The Guardian* newspaper in August 2016, "If the world puts all its resources into finding ways to generate power without burning fossil fuels, and if there were international agreements that action must happen instantly, and if carbon emissions were brought down to zero before 2050, then a rise of no more than 1.5C [degrees Celsius] might just be achieved." He added, "That is a tall order, however." If the world does warm to 1.5 degrees Celsius, there will still be considerable impacts – but warming to 2 degrees Celsius could mean more extreme storms, droughts, floods and heat waves, degradation of coral reefs, and permanent inundation of some coastal areas and islands.[24]

The impacts of climate change have been and will be felt around the world. In 2014, an IPCC report warned that no one is safe from the impacts of climate change. According to a United Nations blog post summarizing the report, "Observed impacts of climate change have already affected agriculture, human health, ecosystems on land and in the oceans, water supplies, and some people's livelihoods. The striking feature of observed impacts is that they are occurring from the tropics to the poles, from small islands to large continents, and from the wealthiest countries to the poorest."[25]

However, some countries will be affected more than others as climate change progresses. In its 2011 Climate Change Vulnerability Index, Maplecroft, a UK-based global risk and strategic consulting firm, lists 16 countries as facing "extreme risk." Asian countries such as Bangladesh, India and Nepal, and African countries like Zimbabwe and Madagascar, populate the list of the top ten countries likely to be most affected. United States, Germany, France and the UK rate two rungs down as "medium risk" countries.[26]

After doing all of this research, we were more sure than ever that the world is hooked on fossil fuels. Major economies are largely dependent on fossil fuels for their energy, and direct and indirect employment in fossil fuel industries is a significant source of jobs. At the same time, global fossil fuel use is a dangerous addiction. Apart from the environmental impacts associated with fossil fuel extraction, transportation and use, burning fossil fuels is warming the planet in a way that may soon cause irreversible changes and make it more difficult or even dangerous for humans and other species to live.

Given these negative impacts, many countries are looking to transition away from the use of fossil fuels. In December 2015, at the end of the United Nations Climate Change Conference held in Paris, nearly 200 countries committed to end the fossil fuel era. Many of these countries committed to deep reductions in their greenhouse gas emissions in a short timeframe, and some committed to increasing their development of renewables. Overall, many countries are talking about making a transition to renewable energy sources.

While some countries that are working on developing renewable sources of energy are motivated by climate change and its impacts, there are other incentives in the mix. Alex L. Wang, a law professor at the University of California, Los Angeles, and an environmental expert on China, explains this point well in the Chinese context. "In recent years, a variety of factors – crisis levels of pollution, economic opportunities from green development and concerns about the domestic risks of rising temperatures – have pushed China to action on climate change," he told *The New York Times* in a 2017 interview.[27]

Irrespective of the motivation, it's clear that renewable energy is expanding rapidly and challenging the fossil fuel industry. A recent Frankfurt School-UNEP Collaborating Centre report states that, in 2015, global investments in renewable sources of electricity more than doubled global investments in new gas and coal electricity generation – US$265.8 billion compared to an estimated US$130 billion. During the same year, 53.6 per cent of all new electricity generating capacity installed that year came from renewable energy (excluding large hydro), making up the majority of additions for the first time ever, and beating fossil fuels.[28]

These developments are definitely positive. It's clear renewable energy is growing globally. But will a transition from fossil fuels to renewables merely represent a shift in the resource providing our daily energy, or will it impact our lives, our livelihoods and the broader communities we live in?

◆

A few months after our conversation with Zoltán, we had the opportunity to take a course at CEU called Sustainable Energy Transitions. The professor teaching the course, Dr. Aleh Cherp, was our MESPOM course coordinator and an expert in energy transitions. In his first, whirlwind lecture, he explained how fossil fuels had helped create the modern world we live in. After his class, we dove into the subject, reading everything we could about it.

We learned that in the past, people across the world were dependent on biomass such as wood and charcoal for all their energy needs. People used biomass as an energy source for cooking and lighting, and for some industrial activities like salt production and iron- and glass-making. The first large-scale energy transition – from biomass to coal – took place in the UK, which had nearly completed this transition by the end of the 18th century. The Industrial Revolution that began in the country in the late 1700s and later spread throughout the world cemented the importance of fossil fuels in modern society.[29]

Energy transition scholars Roger Fouquet and Peter Pearson give a straightforward definition of energy transitions as "a switch from an economic system dependent on one or a series of energy sources and technologies to another."[30] Following the UK, all the world's major economies, including the United States, Germany, France, Russia, Japan, China and India, made the classic transition from biomass to coal, albeit on different timelines. China and India began the transition most recently, and some people in parts of both of these countries still rely on biomass. In many of the world's major economies, the transition to coal has been followed by a transition to hydrocarbons such as oil, and then natural gas. Overall, by the end of the 20th century, the world had transitioned from biomass to fossil fuels as the dominant fuel. Biomass was almost eliminated – except in some rural areas of poor countries.[31]

We wanted to know how these past transitions had happened and how they had impacted people and societies. We were looking for clues that could help us understand how the next big transition – from fossil fuels to renewable energy – could take place, and how it would impact people.

We looked at the example of the UK. Before the Industrial Revolution in the UK, human lives were very different. Prior to the industrial era, people used biomass, including wood and crop residues, for cooking, lighting and other domestic purposes. For transportation, people relied on animals, travelled on foot or harnessed the power of wind to propel ships.[32] This all changed with one important invention that made the large-scale use of coal possible: the steam engine. In 1769, James Watt patented an improved, efficient steam engine that ran on coal.[33] The first widespread use of this efficient steam engine was to pump water out of coal mines, making coal seams easier to access. Thanks to this, miners could extract more coal, enabling the expansion of coal use. The increased availability of coal, in addition to the new, efficient steam engine, helped industries – including the iron, pottery, brick, glass, cotton and steel industries – expand production.[34]

In the pre-industrial era, most people worked in agriculture as farmers or as other food producers such as fishermen and hunters. As industrialization spread, many people left agriculture and migrated to become factory workers. This shift in occupation was widespread.[35] The wages of these new factory workers were much higher than their previous earnings as farmers. This drove increased consumption, which resulted in demand for more goods, further supporting the growth of industry.

Overall, the Industrial Revolution created new wealth and led to the expansion of a new industrial workforce. The quality of human life improved for many people, more food was available where previously there had been scarcity, and advancements were made in every field – for example, in medicine.

The UK example helped us understand how the development of modern society was based on fossil fuels. It also helped illustrate how past energy transitions had created new worlds, altering societies and bringing about rapid changes in people's lives. Past transitions have had a huge impact on communities and livelihoods. We understood that if and when a transition to renewable energy comes, it may create similar large-scale changes in our societies.

Some experts believe that the coming renewable energy transition will mean a shift from a more command-and-control-style energy system to a more participatory one. Stanford professor and energy expert Tony Seba puts this quite eloquently in his book, *Clean Disruption of Energy and Transportation*. "The [fossil fuel] energy industry is a hierarchical, command-and-control world. Big Banks invest in Big Energy Assets that Big Utilities operate to sell energy to individuals, families and businesses. Energy flows one way (from Big Energy to the user) and cash flows the opposite way (from the user to Big Energy)."[36]

On the other hand, he states that renewable energy and related technologies, which he refers to as "clean disruption," "will be about abundant, cheap and participatory energy." In a participatory energy system, people and communities will participate in production, distribution, transmission and storage of their energy.[37] For example, in several countries, individuals with personal solar arrays that provide energy to their homes can sell excess electricity back to the grid. In this way, many individuals participate in the overall production and provision of energy. This is one illustration of how a new renewable world could look very different than our current fossil fuel reality.

After our research, we still had big questions. We knew we couldn't learn everything from behind a desk and that we had to see first-hand how this was playing out in the real world. We wanted to know how the fossil fuel industry was impacting people on the ground in our home countries of India and Canada. Were governments truly serious about the urgent need to transition from fossil fuel dependency towards renewable energy – and what were they doing about it? Apart from government action, what innovations were driving the creation of a renewable energy world? Was there any plan in place to help guide this total transition, and to help retrain current fossil fuel workers in other industries? And if government wasn't ready to help in this area, could the initiative come from the ground up?

By the end of June 2016, when our first year of MESPOM ended, we had completed our preliminary research and had a successful crowdfunding campaign under our belt. It was time to head to the coal mining belt in the eastern Indian state of Jharkhand to hear peoples' stories and find some answers.

*Part II*

---

# JOURNEY TO JHARKHAND

## Chapter Three

# THE COAL-CYCLE *WALLAH*

*I spend all week with my family, scavenging coal from the nearby mine... my whole family is involved.*
—Raju Munda, coal-cycle *wallah*

Giriraj Kumar pauses and prays to Kali, the Hindu goddess of death, each time he enters the underground coal mine. On a beam at the mine's threshold hangs a framed, faded picture of Kali holding a sickle and a man's severed head. Giriraj, the young overman of the Argada underground coal mine in central Jharkhand, told us that no major accidents had happened in the four years he had overseen the mine, "Thanks to God." Despite his luck, conditions inside the mine are frightening.

Following Giriraj, we descended 30 smooth, stone steps into the dark mine, each of us using only a sharp, pointed, wooden walking stick to keep our balance. Groundwater ran along the steps in some places, making the path slippery. Inside the mine, the steps steeply descended into unlit gloom. We used hand-held flashlights roped to our bodies to light the way. Giriraj told us that the mine extends down a kilometre and a half, and around 400 people work there – about 75 per shift. There is no elevator. Day after day, mine workers must walk down the slippery steps in darkness to the depths of the mine to extract coal. A mechanical pulley drags railway carts laden with extracted coal to the surface. The painstaking labour that these workers perform each day to chip coal out of the depths of the earth supplies the raw material that power plants consume by the truckload to produce electricity for Indian households.

Hours before meeting Giriraj at the Argada mine, we were

in Religara, an open-cast mine in the same region. Open-cast is the more common type of coal mining in India. It takes place above ground. When a coal seam – imagine an underground river of coal – is close enough to the surface, it is cheaper and faster to mine it using open-cast methods. Workers first blast the surface with explosives to loosen it up, then dig out and remove the surface vegetation and the top layer of soil. This material, called the "overburden," is piled in heaps near the mine. Workers then remove the coal close to the surface by digging, blasting to loosen the coal, and excavating it.

Religara looked like an asteroid had hit Earth and exploded, creating a huge crater and spilling piles of coal and overburden in every direction. The area appeared devastated. Large dump trucks drove up and down muddy access roads just wide enough to fit them, transporting huge chunks of coal removed from the active face of the mine below. We visited Religara mine with Arun Kumar Singh, a trade union leader and an elected member of the *panchayat* (local government). "Look at that road," he fumed as a dump truck trundled past. "It's so narrow. If there was an accident, that dump truck and its driver would go over the face of the cliff." Arun told us that there are many critical safety issues with mines in this region, and standards are lax. We walked along the main access road to the workers' rest hall, which stood on a flat area at the top of the mine. "Just this year, someone died under a dump truck right here," he said, pointing to the road that led down into the mine. "Now they have built some basic fences to cordon off areas where workers often stand."

Both underground and open-cast coal mining in India are dangerous. Although Giriraj claimed he hadn't seen any accidents in his time at the Argada underground mine, an analysis of a recent annual report by Coal India Limited (CIL), the owner of the Argada mine, reveals that, on average, a coal miner has died every three days for the past 40 years in India.[38] During Sandeep's career as a journalist, one of his first assignments as a reporter for the *Daily News & Analysis (DNA)* newspaper was to investigate coal mining deaths. Through his research, he discovered that the picture is actually much worse: on average, a coal miner dies every day. The official numbers are grossly under-reported because coal mining companies do a poor job of recording the number of deaths.[39] For example, sometimes contractors don't report to CIL the deaths of contract workers who die on the job, which means these deaths don't show up in CIL's official death statistics. And it's not just fatalities. Although CIL claims it is constantly improving mining safety, more than 5,000 workers suffered serious injuries in the last 40 years: some lost their hands; others became paralyzed.

One reason for these accidents is the lax safety standards that Arun described. "While all the mechanisms are in place, proper safety procedures are not always followed by the company," Arun said. India has a standing committee on safety in coal mines, made up of CIL officials and trade union representatives and headed by the federal minister of coal. At every meeting, someone raises coal mine safety as an issue. B.K. Rai, vice president of a prominent coal industry trade union, raised the issue in a March 2015 committee meeting. Upset about the poor quality of safety equipment, he said, "Substandard quality safety equipment like cap lamp, and shoes are being provided to the workers and officials which was a serious compromise on the front of safety."[40] Despite some improvements, Indian coal mines remain very unsafe for workers. Recently, as the world prepared to celebrate New Year's Eve at the end of 2016, an open-cast coal mine collapsed in Jharkhand, killing 23 miners.[41]

The dangerous coal mining industry is responsible for producing about 70 per cent of the total electricity used in India today. And the Indian government is dependent on coal for more than just electricity generation. To start with, the government owns most of the coal industry. Coal mining in India used to be done mainly by private operators, but in the early 1970s, the government of India started to nationalize the coal industry. Today, CIL, the government coal company, operates

430 mines and produces 84 per cent of the coal in the country. The company is highly profitable, reporting yearly increases in net profits, and it has plans to grow. A few private companies remain, but they are very small compared to CIL. Overall, the government of India is still sitting on approximately 300 billion tons of coal, the fifth-largest proven coal reserves in the world, and it has plans to continue expanding coal mining in the country.[42] The federal government has set a target to double coal production from the current five million tonnes per year to one billion tonnes per year by 2020.[43]

Coal India Limited is also a massive employer in India. The company operates in nine Indian states, including Jharkhand, and directly employs about 300,000 people, making it the world's largest coal mining company. However, it has now outsourced a large portion of its operations to private contractors, which greatly expands the number of workers. Ramendra Kumar, a former member of parliament and a prominent trade union leader in the coal industry, told us, "It is hard to estimate exactly how many workers work indirectly for Coal India. However, as per various estimates, Coal India directly or through contractors employs more than 500,000 people in the country."

For CIL employees, working conditions are poor. For contract workers, conditions are even worse. "The contract workers are poorly paid, and don't have any medical or retirement benefits," Ramendra told us. In addition to CIL's employees, millions of people are indirectly dependent on the coal industry. In India, small townships have developed near every coal mine, where people run shops, hotels and other businesses that provide services to coal workers. These townships are also home to poor villagers who scavenge for coal and sell it for their survival. It's indisputable that the coal industry is responsible for feeding millions of Indians. When we passed through Gidi, the town near the Argada mine, there were hundreds of small shops selling everything from live chickens to sweets and tea. We stopped at one such shop with Arun, and he insisted on treating us to some *rasgulla* (a sweet, milk-soaked dumpling) and chai.

While workers' issues are one part of the story, the coal industry in India is also marred by rampant corruption and poor environmental practices. In 2012, a huge scam came to light in India's coal industry. Starting in 1991, a series of federal governments began allocating coal blocks (areas for coal mining) to private companies. The problem was that they allegedly allocated some blocks to favoured companies, and allocated others randomly. All of this was done without criteria and without a bidding process. This means the government likely lost out on large potential profits that could have been generated by competitive coal block auctions. In August 2012, the comptroller and Auditor General of India tabled a report in the Indian parliament claiming that the arbitrary allocation of coal blocks led to a total loss of Rs 1.86 lakh crore (about US$33 billion) in taxpayer's money. That's more than the money required to feed the 870 million undernourished people in the world every year.[44] The investigation into the scam is ongoing, along with multiple court cases.

Degradation of land and water is another important issue associated with the coal industry, and likely the most ignored. There are many examples. When Sandeep was working for the DNA newspaper, he investigated CIL and discovered that the company had mined, destroyed and abandoned at least 600 square kilometres of land – roughly the size of Greater Mumbai – across the nine states it operates in.[45]

On our way to Gidi, where the Argada mine is located, we saw several abandoned mines. "The abandoned land could be reclaimed and used to set up new projects. But nobody is talking about the way the land is left, let alone what should be done with it," Sandeep said.

"Aren't there laws that require the mine operators to reclaim the mine?" Savannah asked. Sandeep explained that according to mandatory government guidelines, once companies are done open-cast mining, they should backfill the excavated area and restore it to its original level within three months. Yet, in practice, nothing happens, and the degraded land is left abandoned.

Sandeep added that despite these issues, coal mining brings significant revenues from royalties for at least six state governments in states where coal mining is prominent. For instance, the state of Jharkhand received Rs 3,170.85 crore (about US$500 million) as royalties from coal mining in the 2015–16 financial year, which is almost 6 per cent of its total state revenues.[46] Despite receiving large profits from coal mining, Jharkhand remains one of the most underdeveloped states in the country. The wealth Jharkhand is making from coal mining simply isn't trickling down to the people. We wondered where all the money goes.

◆

When we arrived in Ranchi, the capital city of Jharkhand, a few days before our visit to the Argada and Religara mines, we saw a bustling city that's developed in a haphazard and unplanned way. Cows munched garbage in steaming piles by the roadside. One sloping, steel-roofed shop rubbed elbows with another, with no parking to be seen.

And in Sandeep's parents' apartment, there were frequent power cuts, often lasting from ten a.m. until four p.m. That meant no internet, no lights, no fridge and no kitchen appliances – though Sandeep's parents had few electric kitchen appliances for just this reason, and cooked on a gas stove. One of the only times Sandeep's mom decided to use an electric blender to make the base of a curry for lunch, the power cut out mid-blend. For the next few hours, she ran to the kitchen, laughing, every time the building's generator briefly kicked in and the electricity came back on. We had lunch around four p.m. that day.

When the power went out unexpectedly, we took it as an unscheduled break from working on the book. We would work as long as our computers had battery charge, and then take the day off when they shut down. Although we enjoyed our breaks, we would surely have felt differently if this were our everyday reality. Somehow Ranchi, the capital of the power-house of India, wasn't supplying adequate power to its own people to light their homes and run their fans.

Yet many people in Ranchi are well-off compared to those living in the rest of the state. For example, hundreds of thousands of families outside cities make their living as coal-cycle *wallahs*; it's the only way they can feed themselves and their families. On our way back from visiting the mines, we drove along Patratu Road, a newly paved, high-quality road that extends out from Ranchi. Jindal Steel and Power Limited, a private company, built the road to ensure smooth transport of its products. The road cuts through swaths of lush green forest with towering sal and eucalyptus trees. This scene is occasionally broken up by vast rice paddies tilled by lungi-wearing farmers. Driving along the road, we began to see small groups of thin men pushing heavily laden bicycles. Each rusty, simple bicycle was packed with bags of coal, roped to the bicycle and sticking out in all directions like an elaborate headdress. The first bicycle we saw had eight medium-sized bags roped to both sides of the front of the bicycle frame, and five roped to either side of the back wheel. There was no chance that its thin, tired-looking owner could actually ride it. Instead, the coal-cycle *wallah* trudged next to the bicycle, slowly pushing it along.

We stopped along the way and got out to speak to one coal-cycle *wallah* who was pushing his bicycle uphill. In Hindi, *wallah* means "someone doing a particular thing." For example, you can have a *dukan wallah* (a shopkeeper), a *khanabanane wallah* (a cook), or an *istri wallah* (someone who comes to your house and irons your clothes). So a coal-cycle *wallah* is someone in the profession of transporting coal on a bicycle. At first, the coal-cycle *wallah* was reluctant to stop and speak to us. He seemed exhausted yet determined to keep pushing his heavily laden bicycle to its destination. After we explained who we were and what we were doing, he paused and rested his bicycle for a moment. He introduced himself as Raju Munda.

Raju told us that he was from Gidi, the small town 60 kilometres away from Ranchi near where the Argada mine is located. "I spend all week with my family, scavenging coal from the nearby abandoned mine," he told us. "My whole family is involved." After the coal is scavenged, his family helps him wash it to eliminate any ash or other debris, and then cook it in burning, smoking piles near their home. This softens the coal and increases its quality so it can be sold for a higher price. Once a week Raju packs his bicycle with 18 or 19 sacks of coal, which weigh about ten kilograms each. This makes his whole bicycle extremely heavy, weighing close to 200 kilograms. Incredibly, the amount Raju carries is a small amount for a coal-cycle *wallah* – many carry more, up to 450 kilograms per bicycle.

By midweek he packs his bicycle with the coal chunks, then gets up at four in the morning the next day and sets out for Ranchi. He pushes his bicycle, laden with coal, nearly 60 kilometres along the shoulder of the highway. Much of the distance is very steep uphill. It is so steep that recently, a new motorcycle *wallah* business has sprung up. Motorcycle *wallahs* have started towing the coal-cycle *wallahs* up some of the largest hills on the route in groups of two or three, tying all of their bicycles to one motorcycle with a rope. The coal-cycle *wallahs* have to pay roughly Rs 100 (about US$1.50) per trip for this service. Many coal-cycle *wallahs* are willing to pay because otherwise they expend a huge number of precious calories pushing their bicycles up the steep hills. When you live hand to mouth, every calorie counts.

After his four a.m. departure, Raju pushes his bicycle for 14 to 15 hours with little rest, until about six or seven in the evening. Then he stops for the night and sleeps by the side of the road in a farmer's field a few kilometres before Ranchi. The next day he wakes up at four again and pushes his bicycle the rest of the way, reaching Ranchi by eight or nine in the morning. This is where his week's hard work culminates. Once he gets there, he sells his coal in the street, sometimes bribing police officers to look the other way. For Raju and his family's difficult work all week, and Raju's intense and arduous trek to Ranchi, he will make only Rs 800 to 900 (about US$12 to 14). After bribes, Raju is typically left with only about US$10. This means that overall, Raju and his entire family are making only about US$1.40 a day from their hard labour – just enough to eke out a basic existence, eating simple food like plain rice for every meal. Once he sells his coal, Raju will either load his bicycle on a bus or ride it back to Gidi – and then start his week's work all over again.

Raju's story opened our eyes to the incredible dependence that many people living in coal mining areas have on the coal industry. Working as a coal-cycle *wallah* is an extremely tough way to make a living, but these coal-cycle *wallahs* have no other option.

After speaking with Raju, we agreed that what we'd seen so far, while shocking, was only part of the story of coal in Jharkhand. We'd heard that some of the most atrocious practices and worst environmental destruction was actually happening far from Ranchi, in a small town called Jharia – where people had been living amidst burning coal fires for decades. The reason? Unscientific coal mining practices in the town, and little government action to douse the fires. While coal fires burn across the world in coal-producing countries, from the United States to China to Indonesia, the Jharia coalfield fire is one of the largest coal mine fire areas in the world.[47] We wanted to speak to people living there to understand what was happening, why the government had never managed to put the fires out and what kept them living in the area. We made plans to head out for Jharia in the next few days to find out for ourselves.

## Chapter Four

# DANTE'S INFERNO, EASTERN INDIA

*Can you imagine New York or Vancouver or New Delhi on fire for 100 years, and still the residents keep living there? This situation you can only see in Jharia.*
   —Ashok Agarwal, local businessman and head of the Jharia Coalfields Bachao Samiti (Save Jharia Coalfield Committee)

Amit Kumar leaned on the horn, swerving around the cars, autos, pedestrians and cows clogging Ranchi's streets in early-morning traffic. Parwaz Khan, the *Hindustan Times* chief photographer and an old friend of Sandeep's, sat in the front seat, looking unfazed. Suddenly, Ranchi's unplanned and crumbling buildings gave way to a high black fence and green garden, with a massive hotel set back from the street. We had arrived at the Park Plaza hotel, one of Ranchi's fanciest lodgings. As Amit, the driver of our rented car, pulled up at the front of the hotel, Sandeep took out an old Nokia cellphone borrowed from his mom and rang up Ashok Agarwal. Ashok, a local businessman, is the head of the Jharia Coalfields Bachao Samiti (Save Jharia Coalfield Committee), which has been fighting to save the people of Jharia for more than a decade. Briefly in Ranchi for a wedding, he would accompany us on the four-hour drive to the town of Jharia.

As we pulled up to the hotel, a portly man emerged from the main doors. Of medium height, Ashok wore dress pants, a red, blue and white striped shirt, thick bifocals and a Hindu red string tied around his wrist. He made up for the complete lack of hair on his head with a full and well-groomed moustache.

Sandeep had met Ashok previously, during his DNA journalism days, for a story on abandoned mines.

Ashok got into the back of the car beside Savannah and Sandeep. After catching up about their families for a few minutes, Sandeep asked, "Sir, what's happening in Jharia right now?" Ashok paused and sighed. Then, staring straight ahead, skin drooping over his eyes, he began to tell us the story of Jharia.

He told us that coal fires in Jharia have been burning for 100 years. "Can you imagine New York or Vancouver or New Delhi on fire for 100 years, and still the residents keep living there? This situation you can only see in Jharia," Ashok said, twisting his many rings in agitation.

Back when we started researching Jharia, we were shocked that fires could start in a town 100 years ago, and get bigger with every passing day, yet no one, including the government, had done much about it. As we were talking to Ashok, questions ran through our minds: How did the coal fires in Jharia start, and how did Jharia get to the state it's in today? How did the situation become so bad? Had government made any efforts to douse the fires? And why were people still living in Jharia?

"One hundred thousand people are sitting directly on top of the fire in Jharia, out of 700,000 in the whole town," Ashok told us. He said that although previous governments had planned to fill the fire area with sand and stabilize it, nothing had happened. Eventually, the government had decided that sand filling couldn't be done and that the area should be evacuated. "The entire place will have to be evacuated – that means 700,000 people. Has the world ever done this? Can it ever think about seven lakh [700,000] people being rehabilitated?"

Ashok turned towards us. "The biggest problem of the government's rehabilitation scheme is that it doesn't have a provision for any livelihood," he told us. "The main reason why a person stays in a particular place is that he has some livelihood. As long as you have a livelihood, you will stay in a place – otherwise you will shift to another place. That is the history of the world! The main reason why people are living on the fire is that they are dependent on the place for their livelihood." He explained that most people living in Jharia make their livelihoods either by working in the coal industry or by scavenging coal from the coalfields or abandoned mines, burning it to make soft coal, and selling it to people to use for cooking – a lot like Raju, the coal-cycle *wallah*. Everyone in the family is involved, including children.

Ashok said that the history of Jharia's coal fires is a tale of government inefficiency and incompetence. Smita Gupta, a senior Indian economist, in a 2013 report titled *Fanning a Fire in Jharia: Reap Windfall Profits and Loot the Coal*, writes that the Jharia fires were first reported in 1916, but they stayed under control until later. The first coal fires in the area were likely natural, or accidentally caused by humans living their normal lives.

There are many coal seams in Jharia – thick rivers of underground coal fairly close to the surface. When a coal seam below the surface of the earth is exposed to air, the carbon in the coal reacts with the oxygen in the air and produces $CO_2$ and heat. The heat ignites the coal seams, causing fires. Human activity can also result in coal fires – for example, when people burn wood near coal seams, and the seams catch fire. The exact reason the Jharia fires started is still not clear.[48]

While fires had existed since 1916, things started to turn for the worse after 1972. That was the year India nationalized coal and created Coal India Limited and its subsidiary, Bharat Coking Coal Limited (BCCL). BCCL became the main coal mining company in the Jharia area. Before the 1970s, the mining was mostly done underground, but then BCCL adopted open-cast methods that involved digging large surface pits to remove only the upper layers of coal. At the same time, most underground mining stopped. The abandoned underground mines should have been filled with sand to keep oxygen out, but they weren't – and, in Smita's words, are now "a labyrinth of open corridors previously occupied by coal seams standing on coal pillars." To make matters worse, BCCL dug open-cast mines near existing underground mines, allowing oxygen to filter into these pre-existing underground labyrinths. This oxygen reacted with the carbon in the exposed coal in the underground mines, and formed heat and $CO_2$. This started a chain of fires that have continued to burn to this day.

While there may have already been fires in the unfilled underground mines, the influx of oxygen from open-cast mining was like throwing gasoline on the mines and lighting a match. Thus, a natural phenomenon – coal fires – became a regional disaster as fires spread through coal seams in the underground mines that stretch into the surrounding area. Since coal seams in the area are often close to the surface of the earth, fires have started to reach people's homes and spring up between city streets. Historical data shows that, by 1986, 97 coal fires were burning in Jharia.[49] As the fires have grown, other government agencies have gotten involved – for example, the former chairman of the Railway Board complained to the federal coal secretary when BCCL mined too close to railway lines, causing fires that threatened the stability of the railway.

While we talked with Ashok in the car, the town of Ranchi faded behind us. The ramshackle sheds and leaning houses of the city gave way to green rice paddies separated by low brick walls. Every once in a while, a stretch of low shacks with metal roofs appeared along the road, selling mouth-watering street food and surrounded by throngs of dogs and goats. We passed five girls and a boy walking to school along the red dirt path next to the road. The girls wore identical light blue shirts and dark blue skirts, and braids tied in loops with ribbon. As we passed over an unfinished brick bridge with half-built walls, Parwaz said, "You see this bridge? They started building it in the year 2000, when Jharkhand separated from Bihar and became its own state. It's been 16 years and it's still not done!" He laughed. "Government *mahaan hai* – the government is amazing."

Ashok laughed. "That's the story of Jharia too! Successive governments have cheated the people of Jharia." He told us that all governments have promised to douse the fires and evacuate people, and we can all witness where those claims stand.

"Sir, what should be done in Jharia?" Sandeep asked.

Ashok didn't hesitate. "People of Jharia are bona fide citizens of this country," he said. "As a government, you have to look after them. How can you abandon them? You have to provide good rehabilitation – they should go happily. Why should they be forced to go over there? Are they criminals?" He shook his head. "As it stands now, people have no voice – they're scared."

A big problem in Jharia is jobs. The population is dependent on coal mining. Ashok told us that as part of rehabilitating and relocating people, the government has to give people livelihoods. He sighed and said, "You want development, you want coal. Very nice. But what will you give in return? The poor people are asking for a chance to get a job, a roof over their heads, two square meals a day, medical facilities. And education for their children. That's all. Is that very difficult to give?"

Since the fires were detected in Jharia more than 100 years ago, successive governments have formed numerous committees to study the problem and propose solutions, none with any success. Before India gained independence, the British government formed a subcommittee to study coal fires and coal-fire-related subsidence (when land collapses after fire burns away the coal beneath it) in the Jharia coalfields. After that, several committees were created to identify measures to douse the fires. The number of nice glossy reports increased steadily, while the fires did the same beneath Jharia. In 1976, about 30 years after India gained independence, the federal government created a subcommittee, led by a top scientist, that conducted an in-depth investigation into the issues of subsidence and fires in coal mining areas and suggested solutions for these issues. The subcommittee gave a detailed report in 1979. This report is gathering dust somewhere in a federal ministry. Later, in the 1980s, the government tried again. They started a World Bank–funded project, the Jharia Mine Fire Control Technical Assistance Project. The consultants responsible for the project submitted a report in 1996, which identified a number of initiatives that the government could take to control the fires. This report, following the tradition set by many great reports before it, is diligently gathering dust somewhere in a federal ministry.

Meanwhile, the people of Jharia began their fight. The late Haradhan Roy, former member of parliament, decided in 1997 that Jharia couldn't wait for the government any longer. He took Jharia's issue to the highest court in the country – the Supreme Court of India – and started a court case demanding that immediate steps be taken to control the Jharia fires and evacuate the affected population. Around the same time, Ashok's NGO, Jharia Coalfields Bachao Samiti, started a similar case, and the two were combined. In 1999, because of these cases, the Supreme Court ordered the Central Mine Planning and Design Institute, the technical wing of CIL, to prepare a master action plan for dealing with the fires, the subsidence and the evacuation and resettlement of people living in the Jharia coalfields. After a decade of deliberation between various stakeholders – CIL, the government of Jharkhand and the federal government of India – the master plan was finally approved in August 2009. It sets out a strategy for dealing with the fires, subsidence problems and resettlement over a period of 10 to 12 years.

In 2016, only five years were left for the full implementation of the master plan, but the progress had been dismal. In March 2016, the federal government admitted in the Indian parliament that while the government's current target was to evacuate 135,852 families by 2021, so far only 5,684 housing units had been built and less than 4,050 families evacuated.[50] Ashok told us that, so far, the government is failing miserably in meeting its own targets. "And when you talk about 700,000 people, what is going to happen? You are talking out of your hat! You have never given any thought to what is going to happen to 700,000 people," he cried.

While the master plan inches forward, the environment and public health continue to deteriorate. Coal mining already affects the environment, and coal fires make the negative impacts on land, water and air even worse: they cause subsidence and render land infertile, contributing to land degradation; along with the mining, they increase the amount of suspended particulate solids, total dissolved solids and some heavy metals in water, making it hazardous for domestic use; they also release dangerous gases like carbon monoxide, carbon dioxide and oxides of nitrogen and sulphur into the air, along with particulate matter (PM), which is detrimental to health.[51] A study found that in one area of Jharia during winter, the concentration of PM10 was as high as about 270 μg/m$^3$ (millionths of a gram per cubic metre) – that's 13.5 times the World Health Organization's standard.[52]

Researchers state that there are many common health issues in areas affected by the Jharia fires, including "lung and respiratory diseases, nervous problems, high blood pressure, and heat stroke." These scientists also state that "coal fire coupled [with] environmental health hazards are presently giving rise to liver diseases and cancer."[53]

Ashok told us that, in Jharia, many people suffer from health problems, and nearly everyone over 40 has some kind of serious health problem. However, although much has been written on the environmental damage and pollution caused by the fires, no comprehensive study has been done to evaluate the impact on people's health in the area.

◆

At some point during the drive, the rice paddies turned into jungle. A few hours later, the greenery began to thin, and we soon pulled into a town. "Jharia – we're here!" said Ashok. The road entering Jharia was unevenly paved, and small buildings clustered haphazardly along both sides. The street was clogged with cars, autos, bicycles, people, street food vendors on wheels, cows, goats, pigs and trash. We took a quick turn to the left along a street so narrow we were sure the car wouldn't make it through, and then a right turn onto a street full of parked motorcycles and a vendor selling *pani puri*, a popular street food made of a crispy shell filled with flavoured water, chutney, spices, potato, onion and chickpea. Amit stopped the car behind the motorcycles and laid on the horn. The street vendor quickly moved out of the way, and four men emerged out of a shadowed doorway to move the motorbikes. Then everyone but Amit quickly piled out. We followed Ashok into a nondescript white building with a chipped and fading yellow metal door framed by a fringe of dried ceremonial mango leaves. Inside, Ashok invited us into a dimly lit office with dirty pink walls and a broken concrete floor.

We sat down in front of Ashok's crowded desk. It was piled with papers and odd objects, including a large ball bearing. A glass cabinet behind the desk held stacks of yellowed, dusty files and several trade show awards. While Ashok took a call on his cellphone in Hindi, we took a look around the office. On the walls hung an eclectic mix of tribal artwork, a picture of the Dalai Lama and prints of works by famous European painters such as Gauguin and Monet, as well as a picture of Ashok smiling in front of Stonehenge.

Ashok went to a cabinet and pulled out a thick, dusty file. "Here's everything my organization has collected about Jharia," he said. Sitting down at the desk, he flipped open the file and began to read the first letter in it, which was heavily underlined in red pen. "This letter says sand stowing [filling mines with sand] should have been done before abandoning the mines," he said. "It was *never* done!" He showed us several government documents that talked about various actions that should have been taken to deal with the fires and the resettlement. "But nothing happens," Ashok said.

Ashok sighed. "People in Jharia are damned if they move and damned if they don't," he told us. He explained that in Belgoria, the place where evacuated residents are supposed to move, living conditions are abysmal, and there is no source of livelihood. Even though some people have moved to Belgoria, every day they have to travel back to Jharia to find work. Some people come on bicycles or motorcycles, and many walk.

It was hard for us to believe that the government would shift these people without any provision for their employment, given their hand-to-mouth existence. Without work, they have no way of providing food for themselves and their families – and unemployment is tantamount to starvation.

"Is there any livelihood plan at all?" Savannah asked.

"There is no livelihood plan at all! Nothing!" Ashok shouted. "You ask the BCCL people, do they have a plan? They are just waiting for a tragedy to happen. Unfortunately, the tragedy that happens here is in small bits and pieces. So that is why there is no massive United Nations cry that makes the whole country start thinking about this issue."

Resettlement has been slow and inefficient. Ashok told us that BCCL, which is in charge of evacuating the area, is playing a waiting game, banking on the fact that, sooner or later, conditions in Jharia will become so bad that people will have to flee – with the company's help or not. "These poor people who have done no crime, other than trying to earn a living for themselves, the government is trying to throw them out along with the overburden. You see, when you expose the coal and you take it out, the topsoil is called overburden. You throw it away."

Ashok sat back in his chair and flipped the file in front of him closed. "You know," he said, "fossil fuel has become a curse now. If there is a transition and you don't retrain workers, there will be massive problems. And the government is incapable of doing it."

After saying *namaste* to Ashok, we hit the road, turning back onto the main street and driving towards the villages near the coalfields on the outskirts of town. These villages are populated by people eking out a living as coalfield workers or coal scavengers, and people there are the hardest hit by pollution from the fires. To get there, we passed through the centre of the town of Jharia. "This whole town exists strictly because of coal," Parwaz said.

◆

Traffic was thick, and suddenly the car stopped completely, right in the middle of a busy market with stalls selling coconuts, fruit, cooked street food and everything else imaginable. Women dressed in brightly coloured sarees – purple, blue, green, gold and silver – filled the road and shopped at the stalls. The road was choked with cars, motorbikes and pedestrians trying to come from all sides in both lanes at once. Huge buses inched forward through the traffic in both directions. "What's happening?" Savannah asked.

"School rush hour," Parwaz replied. "Get ready to wait at least 20 minutes to go the next 100 metres." As traffic inched forward, we realized that it wasn't actually school rush hour holding up the traffic. The communal garbage pile from the market had spilled out onto the street, turning the road into a one-way. Vendors and shoppers continued to throw coconut rinds, plastic packaging, pineapple tops, baskets, broken phones and other debris onto the new pile on the road. Six cows stood on top of it, munching on the garbage, as motorcycles drove over the trash heap and swerved to avoid them.

"What's happening here?" Savannah asked.

"There's no functioning trash collection in Jharia," said Sandeep. "And no one is bothered to try to fix the problem – most people are struggling to survive day to day. Actually, they are numb. And the government is either corrupt, or incompetent, or both."

Parwaz laughed in the front seat. "You know," he said, "In India, a 'save cows' campaign would work, but never a 'save people' campaign. Save cows, not save people."

Finally, we got past the trash pile and drove through the city towards Lodhna, a small semi-urban area in Jharia. As the streets became narrower and narrower, the houses became poorer and poorer. Most of the houses were low-lying mud shanties. Their outer walls were covered in seashell-shaped, hand-imprinted clumps of dung that the inhabitants were drying to use as fuel. They would chip the dung off the outside of the houses when it was ready to be used in the cooking fire. Piles of scavenged coal burned by the side of the road, part of the softening process to sell the coal as cooking fuel. The air was gritty and thick with smoke.

We drove into a central traffic circle with a raised pedestal intended for police to stand on and direct traffic. The pedestal was vacant except for four black goats sleeping. "Hey – that's Santosh!" Sandeep said, pointing to a man in a white shirt waiting near the traffic circle on a motorbike. Sandeep knew Santosh, a local trade union leader in his early 30s, from his journalism days. Santosh had agreed to show us the area.

With Santosh as our guide, we set out to visit Jharia's outlying Kumhar *basti* (settlement), which had been badly affected by the fires. Santosh and his friend, Shankar Paswan, piled into the back seat. As we drove, the paved road turned into a red dirt track, and the small shanty shops of Lodhna faded away. The track turned towards a small settlement near a stream, and we stopped the car just short of a small bridge. As we got out, schoolchildren walking along the track turned to stare at us. The shallow stream, where people were bathing, was choked with trash. "That's not garbage in water," Parwaz said. "That's water in garbage."

The air had a pungent chemical smell, a mix between garbage and burning plastic. We headed towards the village and started to climb a narrow dirt path winding between unlit low-lying houses of brick and mud. The air was very hot. A thin woman wearing a saree called out to us from her house as we walked past, inviting us for breakfast. We thanked her but carried on. As we walked through the village, the air thickened and became more difficult to breathe. Two minutes of walking brought us to the back of the village, where we saw a black, lunar landscape – an abandoned open-cast mine. It stretched out as far as the eye could see, with only a few grey paths, marked by small piles of coal, across its expanse. Massive coal fires burned close to the village, sending huge plumes of white smoke and gas up into the air. At the margin of the village, where we stood, a man sat next to 15 burlap sacks full of coal. With blackened hands, he banged a rock on pieces of coal to break them apart, placing the small pieces in a sack. He didn't look up as we arrived. As we stood looking out at the mine, a large, nearby coal fire blew clouds of smoke and gas directly onto us.

The same woman who had called out to us in the village came walking towards us with a fierce stare. No more than four feet, ten inches tall, she looked like she weighed less than 40 kilograms. Her purple saree was stained and wrinkled, and she had a large white bandage around one of her thin ankles. With her hair tied back in a bun, we could see that her brown face was creased with deep wrinkles, and her eyes were lively and intelligent. She started to speak rapidly in Hindi to Santosh.

Savannah poked Sandeep. "Hey, can you translate?" Savannah had learned a little bit of Hindi before coming to India but could only catch a few words. Sandeep translated most of the time.

Sandeep frowned for a moment. "Her name is Urmila Devi. She's saying, 'Talk to me! I have something to tell you.'" Urmila told us that she is 50 years old and has two sons – but used to have three. The third son died of gas poisoning seven years ago. One day he came home and told her he'd been exposed to a lot of gas from the fires that day. He lay down and never got up. The other two sons are 18 and 20 and work as daily wage labourers in the town centre. They go there every day in search of work, such as loading and unloading coal onto transport vehicles. If they find work, they eat that day – and if they don't, the whole family goes hungry. Urmila told us she makes money by scavenging coal in the abandoned mine and selling it. Her husband is so sick from the fires that he can't work anymore as a daily wage labourer, so he went away to live with her daughter in a different area. We asked Urmila if she wants to be evacuated to Belgoria.

She laughed, and a growing group of villagers surrounding us chuckled. "I haven't got an offer to go to Belgoria so far! They surveyed, but nothing has happened. In any case, I wouldn't want to go, because there are no jobs. How can I survive there?" She told us she's reluctant to leave because she can make income scavenging coal here in Kumhar *basti*. However, life in the *basti* is unbearable. The drinking water is abysmal. It comes from an underground source near the village and emerges piping hot and full of gases and other particles. It makes them feel sick. They wash their clothes and bodies in the river, but because it's so polluted it makes them feel very itchy. She scratched her stomach to demonstrate.

Santosh motioned us back into the village. A large group of curious adults and watchful children accompanied us as we walked down the narrow, twisting path between houses. Sandeep whispered to Savannah, "This might be the first time they've seen someone who looks like you!" The air was thick and cloudy and smelled strongly astringent, like something no human should ever breathe. We soon came to a low-lying compound with a small metal door framed by a green curtain.

"Come!" said Santosh.

Entering the compound, we saw two houses inside the small mud area: one ground-level house on the left, and one elevated house with steps on the right. Urmila called out to someone in one of the houses, and after a few seconds a young man came down the stairs to join our throng. He was very thin, with a shock of black hair and dark brown skin. He wore only a short lungi. He introduced himself as Parshooram Yadav, 22 years old. Parshooram told us that two or three years ago fire sprouted from the floor of his house.

He motioned us towards the ground-level house on the left,

and we peered inside, surrounded by what must by now have been half the settlement. The heat was oppressive. The floor of the small mud room that made up half the house was covered in drying clumps of coal scavenged from the abandoned mine. A plume of white smoke and gas rose from the floor in the corner. The temperature inside must have been at least ten degrees hotter than the 30 degrees outside, and all of our faces ran with sweat.

"We only cook and dry coal here now," he said. "I had to shift to my sister's house because we couldn't live here anymore. Because of living here, I suffer from headache, nausea and fever. When it rains, it's so polluted I can't breathe." At that moment, a few drops of rain started to fall. "And there is lots of land subsidence... even as we're talking, the ground we're standing on could collapse." We looked at our feet and each other, horrified. We couldn't believe the danger Parshooram and others in the *basti* live in.

He explained that although people in the village are very sick, it's hard for them to see a doctor, as they have to borrow money to go to the hospital. As we talked, clouds of poisonous smoke billowed into the village from the nearby fires. We asked Parshooram if he wanted to move to Belgoria. He frowned. "I don't want to go to Belgoria," he said. "I have been there – but it's dangerous at night. I was beaten up." A few of the other young men standing around nodded in agreement. "There is also no work for us there," he added.

As we left the house, it started to pour outside. We ran, along with a pack of people from the settlement, towards the central square. Sandeep, Parwaz and Santosh sheltered under someone's veranda, while Shankar motioned Savannah towards a central pavilion with gods painted on it, and kicked off his shoes. After Savannah did the same, she stepped up into the pavilion. "This is good," said Shankar. "Maybe the rain will clear some of the gas out before it turns into steam." It became slightly easier to breathe. "This is the temple," said Shankar.

Three small boys had also taken shelter there. "Hello," said

Savannah to the oldest one, who had short black hair and scars on his face that looked like they came from chickenpox. In Hindi, she asked: "*Aap kaise hai* – how are you?"

"*Theek* – okay," he replied, smiling shyly.

"Look at his hand," said Shankar. The boy's hand dangled from the wrist, lifeless, like a piece of rubber. "It's paralyzed because of the pollution," said Shankar.

The rain reduced to a drizzle. We walked back to the river. An astringent smell still hung in the air. "I felt nauseous from that gas after only half an hour" said Savannah. "It's clear they have little choice... but they're really living in hell."

Santosh overheard her. "Here, people live to only 50 or 60. I don't know anyone in their 80s," he said. As we drove away, everyone was quiet in the car, all of us feeling a heaviness in our hearts.

"Everywhere, fathers leave their children with money and property. In Jharia they leave their children with illness and a life of suffering," Shankar said after a few moments.

Bumping along the red dirt track, mining overburden piled on either side, we saw the words HAPPY NEW YEAR written on the top of one of the discarded piles of mining overburden, 40 metres up. The words were made of large white stones that stood out in stark contrast to the black overburden. "Where did that come from?" Sandeep asked.

"The local boys went up one night and wrote it," Shankar said. He paused for a minute and then looked at us with a small smile. "You know, we may have nothing. But you will not see us any less in life. We are full of life."

◆

Jharia faded away into pure greenery on both sides of the road. There were few settlements. We stopped several times to ask for directions, and finally came to a fork in the road. One of the forks was a dirt track that ran off to the left. A man and woman standing by the side of the road directed us towards the dirt track. As we drove down it, blocky, uniform apartment buildings began to appear, a settlement eked out in the middle of nowhere. We'd arrived in Belgoria, the township that the government was building to relocate people from the Jharia fire zone. The apartment buildings were all identical – four or five stories, painted in uneven shades of grey and yellow. We stopped in a central area and piled out of the car. Two men sat there on plastic chairs. A man with dark brown skin, a thick shock of curly hair and a big red necklace introduced himself as Mohan Bhuiyan. The other man, who was very tall, introduced himself as S.P. Singh. Santosh had connected us with Mohan earlier that day.

They led us into one of the big buildings. The apartments were basic, made completely of concrete and brick, and looked new. We climbed a set of stairs and stopped outside an apartment door. Mohan led us in, motioning first for us to take off our shoes. The first room of the apartment had a tiny kitchen, and the second room, painted dark green, had a single wooden bed with a mattress on top; a laundry line laden with clothes stretched across the room. The air smelled fresh. A pair of underwear hung on the top of the bedroom door and a pink tube marked *Clear Skin*, complete with its packaging, was stuck to the middle of one dark green wall as decoration.

A short man wearing a white formal shirt and blue pants stood inside the room. He introduced himself as Ohmprakash Bhuiyan, the owner of the apartment. He held a green hard hat in one hand, and his face was creased with worry. He motioned for us to sit down on the bed, the only piece of furniture in the room. He told us that he moved to Belgoria in 2010, and before that he lived in a settlement next to the coalfields called Golakd *basti*. Life was bad in Golakd. He suffered from headaches and tuberculosis and "choked on the air."

He told us that the air is much better in Belgoria, but the water supply and quality is unpredictable. And while Belgoria is clean now, it won't stay clean for long – open sewer lines lie outside; some for the last two years. There's also no trash pickup. He beckoned us to his balcony and said, "See the view." The ground between the flats was covered in a sea of garbage.

Despite all this, he echoed the consistent theme that we'd heard throughout the day: that the biggest problem in Belgoria is that there are no jobs and no means to make a livelihood. If you're one of the few lucky ones to find any employment, it's only temporary construction work building the houses. Ohmprakash told us that he, like most people in Belgoria, travels 13 kilometres back to Jharia each day for work – returning to the same dangerous place he left to move to here. Some days he walks and some days he rides a bicycle. There's no public transport, and Ohmprakash can't afford a vehicle.

He told us Jharia is the only place in practical range where people can find work; he works there as a stone picker for R.K. Mines, a contractor working for BCCL. "If there was work here, everything would be better," Ohmprakash told us. "We're so desperate for work."

And there are other issues. There's a primary school in Belgoria and a government school, but no teachers go to the government school, so no students go there either. They have no doctor, no medical facilities, no police and no funeral facilities. When someone dies, the body has to be taken 13 kilometres back to Jharia by whatever means possible – and it costs roughly Rs 1500 (about US$23), a large chunk of the average worker's monthly salary. Many are unemployed in Belgoria, and sometimes there are incidents between people, but the last time residents tried to call the police, it took them eight hours to come. Ohmprakash told us that what they needed most is employment and education – then the living situation in Belgoria would be bearable.

"Ashok was right. People are really damned if they move here and damned if they don't," Savannah said to Sandeep. "In Jharia, people are dying slowly from the pollution and living conditions, but in Belgoria they have no way to feed themselves and their families."

"How were people moved to Belgoria?" Savannah asked,

with Sandeep translating. Mohan, leaning against the wall, told us that the government had conducted a survey, and some people had received a card. Eventually, a small number of families were offered flats in Belgoria. They were also offered Rs 10,000 (about US$155) for moving. They were very concerned about employment, so the government offered them 500 days of minimum-wage employment. They were also promised Rs 60,000 (a little more than US$926) to make up for any employment gap. However, when they got to Belgoria, the Jharia Rehabilitation and Development Authority (JRDA) deducted Rs 30,000 (about US$463) of that money for things like electricity and water connections. They also pay JRDA Rs 100 (about US$1.50) per month in rent.

It all adds up, Mohan told us – but if they could just get employment, life would be better. He told us that some people came to Belgoria but couldn't handle the unemployment, decided that life was better in Jharia and returned there. Sandeep asked Mohan whether he is happy that he came to Belgoria. Mohan thought for a moment. "It's a dilemma."

Mohan and S.P. explained that we were visiting one of the older buildings, but we should really see one of the new ones. They told us the newer buildings have been very poorly constructed, using low-quality materials. We walked along the red dirt road next to the apartment blocks. The ground-floor apartment lawns were fringed with chicken wire doubling as laundry line. Mohan told us there had been many suicides in Belgoria – at least 12 or 13 in the previous year, all unemployed young men.

We got to one of the new apartment blocks, which looked ten years older than the "old" apartment we had just visited, and had clearly been made from different material. There were visible cracks in the walls. Mohan alleged that the new apartments were constructed with low-grade material because the building contractor was corrupt and saved a lot of money (that went into his own pocket) by using sand and mud as primary building materials instead of concrete. As we climbed the stairwell, S.P. easily broke off a chunk of wall with his hand, covering us with a shower of gritty sand and dust.

We met a family standing in an empty flat with water covering the floor. "The pipes are leaking already," S.P. told us, "and wait until you see the roof." We climbed to the roof and saw that the water tank there had already sprouted five or six small leaks. "But look at the next roof," said S.P., pointing to another tank gushing water. "That is like a little Ganges! You can start growing crops." From the top of the building, S.P and Mohan showed us deep cracks in the walls. They told us that the people in the building are afraid that if there's an earthquake, the building will collapse and they'll be crushed – but they have no option but to live there. As we went downstairs, S.P. told us, "Everyone will die here. It's a place of death – the building will collapse."

◆

Later that afternoon, we had an appointment with the government agency responsible for Belgoria and the Jharia resettlement plan – the JRDA – and intended to confront them with the numerous questions we had after seeing the conditions in Belgoria. The JRDA is the government agency responsible for administering the government's master plan to save Jharia. Its office is in a small compound off a main street in Dhanbad, the administrative capital of the Jharia region. As we walked through the main doors, we saw a small Styrofoam model of Belgoria on the floor to our left, looking like a 6th-grade science project. The doorman ushered us into a large office directly to the left of the door. Gopal Ji, the rehabilitation and resettlement officer of the JRDA – a heavy-set man with grey hair dyed red with henna – sat behind a large wooden desk. Yellow-green shower curtains with floral patterns acted as drapery, shading two windows to the side and behind his desk. There were towels everywhere – a towel beneath his cellphone, a towel over an unused computer screen behind him, and a towel on the back of his chair. The room was hot, and he used the cellphone towel periodically to wipe his face. Three rows of three chairs each sat in front of his desk.

We sat in the first row. Sandeep told Gopal Ji that we'd just visited Belgoria, where the main problem workers brought up was unemployment – they can't live there without any source of livelihood. He asked what the JRDA is doing to address this problem. Gopal Ji covered his face with his hands and leaned back in his chair. His fingers were covered in rings. He flung his hands away from his face and shouted, "No, no, no! We will *not* provide any employment for these people. That is very clear!"

He shifted in his seat and told us it's impossible to provide employment for so many people. At the most, the agency can provide the people of Jharia with better housing – but employment is not its responsibility. "We're providing training to people there, but beyond that, nothing else can happen." He wiped his face with the cellphone towel. "You know," he said, "every time we do a survey in Jharia, we find the number of people has increased manyfold. When we did the first survey, there were about 24,000 households, but now it's increased to about 93,000 or probably more."

We asked whether he thinks Jharia will be evacuated quickly. "*Kachua ka chal mein* – as slow as a tortoise," he replied. "In my view, there is a deadlock, and the rehabilitation process will happen very, very slowly."

"What's the biggest problem you face in rehabilitating these people?" Savannah asked.

"Our biggest issue is that we're not able to acquire land for construction of new buildings," Gopal Ji replied. "Although BCCL has already acquired some land, we're not able to acquire further fresh land. Some farmers are protesting that they don't want to give up their land for the resettlement. So we're not able to do fast rehabilitation."

Savannah asked him how many letters he's issuing each month to invite people from Jharia to move to the new flats in Belgoria. He gave a rough estimate of 20 to 25 letters each month, but said, "It's not fixed." He told us that it doesn't matter much anyway because "people don't want to move out of their old homes. Even today, 500 apartments are lying unoccupied." We thought back to the crumbling apartments in Belgoria.

Sandeep asked when the resettlement would be completed. Gopal Ji sighed and leaned back in his chair. "The project should be completed by 2021, but let's see when it will get completed," he said.

There was movement at the back of the room. As we looked behind us, dozens of people poured into the room and started sitting down in the chairs around us. They had come from Jharia to ask for apartments.

## Chapter Five

# A COAL WORKER'S DIARY

*We have been dependent on the coal industry for generations now. But now this very coal has become a curse for us.*
        —Suresh Bhuiyan, a coal worker from Jharia

Srikumari Devi has pain in her knees, and her eyes are always burning. While throbbing knees and watering eyes have become part of her life, every now and then she suffers from high fevers, colds, lung problems and diarrhea. Ill health has been her constant companion for the last decade. When we met Srikumari, she was dressed traditionally in an orange and yellow striped saree, its borders embroidered with hundreds of small flowers. Her dark brown hands were like a coffee-coloured river flowing under an orange bridge covered in flowers. Her wrists were adorned with stripes of green, red and white bangles, and she draped her head with the saree, leaving enough of her forehead bare to show the vermilion in the part of her hair. Indian women put a red or red-orange cosmetic powder in the front inch of their hair parting to indicate that they are married. Srikumari looked frail and tired, older than her 51 years. She was hesitant to speak with us. When she spoke, she whispered, "We are in a lot of pain. We have nothing, and our house has been flooded with water." After marriage, Srikumari had lived her whole life in Golakd *basti*, one of the settlements in Jharia badly affected by coal fires.

As we drove to Golakd earlier that morning, the air was smoky. En route, we passed small houses with low stone walls around them. The walls were made of a mixture of stone and coal – coal was so plentiful here that people were using it as a building material. When the road turned into a muddy track and then ended at a large pond ringed by houses, we knew we had arrived in Golakd. The first thing that hit us was the smell. The air was hot, smoky, dusty and sharp, although not as choked as in Kumhar *basti*. Savannah leaned down and touched the ground with her palms. "It's hot," she said as Sandeep and Parwaz wiped their foreheads. Stray dogs, pigs and chickens were moving freely around the village, defecating everywhere. As we walked into Golakd *basti*, a group of pigs of all sizes tussled in a drain by the pond.

The pond is the main feature of the *basti*. About 15 metres across and the same distance wide, the water is bright green at the edges. A ditch that runs through the village drains directly into the pond, and when we arrived it stank like garbage. That didn't deter six large cows from relaxing right in the middle of the pond. Women were washing clothes and dishes in the pond, and small children were washing their faces.

The living conditions in the *basti* were miserable and inhumane. It made us wonder what keeps people here. Do they really have no other option? How can the government let them suffer like this – aren't they citizens of India, with basic human rights? We were grappling with these questions when we met Srikumari's husband, Suresh Bhuiyan, for the first time. A thin and frail man with short black hair, a weathered face and reddened eyes, Suresh was talkative and outspoken, unlike Srikumari. He wore a dirty shirt with yellow and grey stripes, and a lungi tucked in at the waist. He was missing several teeth, and those that remained were stained a deep brown.

The first thing Suresh told us was that the underground coal fires and resultant pollution and subsidence have wreaked havoc in his family's lives. The *basti* is sandwiched between coal operations on all four sides: by an operational open-cast coal mine on one side, coal mining overburden on the other, and railway cart coal loading operations on the final two. Dust and polluted air enter the village from every direction, making the lives of the 800 residents in the *basti* very difficult.

Suresh told us that, along with his family, he used to live

in the house right next to the pond. Three years back, dirty water from the pond flooded their house. Suresh, Srikumari and their other family members tried to clear the water several times but failed. When we met Suresh, he was still trying to brush water out of the house with a *jhadu* (a coconut-frond broom). The house had muddy walls framing three tiny rooms. It had no doors. The clay-tiled roof was peaked and gently sloping.

Sandeep asked Suresh how his house flooded and where he lives now. Suresh explained as he continued to brush water from the house. "The underground fires burnt the coal lying below my house, the land subsided, and the level of my house went below the level of the pond." Since Suresh's house had no doors, water from the pond had an easy ride into the house.

When the flooding happened, Suresh, Srikumari, their two younger daughters and their son moved to a house right across the path, where their eldest daughter lived with her husband and three kids. Suresh's family has been living there ever since. "We destroyed a room from my old house, and used the materials to create a room in my son-in-law's house," Suresh told us.

Although Suresh and his family have moved to the new house, their problems have not ended. Fires have worsened in the area, and his family members get sick often. As we continued talking, he stopped sweeping and motioned for us to follow him. About ten metres down the path, Suresh knocked on his neighbour's door. A teenage boy with long hair and a round face came out and greeted us. The boy brought plastic chairs, and soon we were sitting outside a bright green house under a steel roof. Suresh said that we should talk here because there was no space for us to sit and talk in his eldest daughter's cramped house. Within minutes, we were surrounded by a group of 20 to 30 people – children, women and men from the village who were curious about our visit. They all were very outspoken and frustrated about the fire situation in the area and the government's apathy towards them.

As Suresh started talking, he was almost in tears. "I am not able to make ends meet. We have a lot of medical expenses because we are constantly exposed to the smoke and poisonous gases that come out of the fires. And every now and then, people in my family get sick."

Sandeep asked Suresh if he gets sick too. Suresh laughed and said, "*Mein amrit nahi peeta hoon* – I don't drink holy water. Of course I get sick." The villagers around us laughed too, but we had a sinking feeling in our stomachs. His face paled. "These coal fires are like slow poison – they are destroying us slowly. Every day."

Every month, Suresh spends about Rs 2,000 to Rs 2,500 (about US$31 to 38) towards his family's medical expenses. "I earn only Rs 7,000 every month [about US$108], and out of that, almost one-third goes towards medical expenses."

Suresh is one of more than 500,000 workers working in India's official coal industry. He works for a private contractor that crushes and transports coal for BCCL. The permanent employees of BCCL get good salaries and other basic facilities, such as free housing, electricity and water. Contract workers like Suresh don't get these benefits. They have no social security net. Even if a permanent employee and a contract worker do the same job, their salaries and other benefits are different. If Suresh were a permanent employee doing the same work he does today, he'd be getting Rs 50,000 (about US$772) every month – about seven times what he currently earns – plus the extra benefits.

In 2013, after years of collective bargaining, coal industry trade unions successfully reached an agreement with Coal India Limited (CIL) management to increase minimum wages and implement social security schemes for contract workers like Suresh. This was a first for any industry in India. Five central coal industry trade unions worked together for many years to make this happen, holding demonstrations and protests and negotiating tirelessly with government. In 2010, after protracted union negotiations, the federal minister of state for coal called a meeting and created a High Power

Committee made up of representatives from CIL and the coal industry trade unions. The committee's objective was to investigate the situation of coal mining contract workers and to make recommendations about their wages and lack of social security measures.

In 2013, the committee recommended that unskilled contract workers like Suresh should get Rs 472 per day (about US$7.30) or Rs 12,272 per month (about US$189) in wages – a little less than double what Suresh currently makes. The committee also recommended that the workers be provided with a pension when they retire, medical care while they're working and a yearly bonus. Finally, it recommended that contract workers receive the same facilities – such as canteens and rest shelters – that CIL's permanent employees receive. These changes sound like a huge improvement. And it would have been a step in the right direction – if it had happened. In the years since, many private contractors across the coal mining industry continue to wilfully ignore the committee's recommendations. The salaries of contract workers like Suresh haven't increased, and they haven't received any other benefits, such as medical care. "We thought our working conditions would get better. But actually they have become worse," said Suresh. Every month, a contribution towards the coal mines pension fund is deducted from his salary, but he claimed that he hasn't received a pension fund receipt so far. "I don't know if it is really getting cut for the pension fund or not," he said.

And Suresh is luckier than others. He at least has a regular job. His son-in-law is a daily wage labourer. "Sometimes he finds work, sometimes he doesn't," Suresh told us. "He goes to town in search of work every day, and on many occasions comes back without any money. The days he finds work, he makes Rs 100 [about US$1.50]." The meagre money that Suresh and his son-in-law earn is used to take care of all their family's expenses – health, food, education and more. Together, they're the only two breadwinners in a family of ten. "Quite often I'm forced to borrow money from my friends. Sometimes I even borrow from moneylenders who charge very high interest rates," said Suresh. The previous month, he'd had to borrow Rs 1000 (about US$15.50) from a friend to pay his son's school fees.

Suresh and Srikumari live a very hard life. Suresh does stone picking work for the private contractor – after an area is blasted to loosen up the coal for mining, he picks stones out of piles of coal. "I have to work 26 days every month – at least ten hours daily," he told us. Since Suresh is a member of the Centre of Indian Trade Unions (CITU), a prominent national-level union, he isn't forced to work for more than ten hours a day. "People who aren't part of the union have to work for up to 15 hours a day," he said.

The first day we met Suresh, he had come back from a six-a.m.-to-four-p.m. stone picking shift. That morning, he and his co-workers had manually removed 700 kilograms of stones. Suresh said that his workplace has no facilities for workers – including no toilets.

The next day, when we came back to meet Suresh, he was getting ready to go to a two-p.m. shift. He told us that he'd gotten up at six a.m. to defecate in the fields and then had gone to take a bath in the *jordia* (lake) one and a half kilometres away. To reach the lake, he had to cross rough terrain and walk through a coal mine. There's no other source of water for bathing, because the pond by Suresh's house is too dirty. The *basti* has one small municipal water tap, which is the only source of drinking water for the 800 inhabitants. Suresh told us that the water only comes out at night for a few hours, and every family gets one or two buckets of drinking water. "Even if we're tired from work, we have to stand in the queue at night for one or two hours to fill water," Suresh said.

"It takes more than one and a half hours to take a bath," he added. And the water in the lake, while better than the pond, isn't clean either – contaminated groundwater unearthed in coal mining operations is disposed of around the mine and often leaches into the lake.

When Suresh came back from the lake that day it was almost eight a.m. Half an hour later, he had breakfast. "We generally eat watery rice with raw chili and onion and salt for breakfast. Only sometimes we can afford to eat *dal* (lentils) and potatoes," he said.

Poor people like Suresh eat the same food every meal. "We can't afford to eat vegetables every day. Sometimes if we have some extra money, then only we're able to eat vegetables," he told us. "The day I have some money, I buy spinach. I really like it a lot. I also like eggplant," he said with a wistful smile.

After having breakfast, he helps his wife with household chores and then has a little extra time to watch TV, which he described as his only source of entertainment. When we met Suresh around 12:45 p.m., he had just finished his lunch – the same watery rice with raw onions and chili that he had in the morning. Suresh's shift would start at two p.m. and go until twelve a.m. He told us that he works without any break during his ten-hour shift. If he's lucky, he gets a five-minute tea break.

If Suresh's life is tough, Srikumari's is no better. She gets up even earlier than Suresh, waking up every day at four a.m., starting the traditional *culha* (hearth), and then going to the fields to defecate. In the *basti*, there's no closed toilet, and for generations the residents have been defecating in the open. In India, women get up very early in the morning to go to the fields so they can avoid potential harassment from men.

Once Srikumari comes back from the fields, she cleans the house, cooks and helps the children get ready to go to school. "I clean the dirty utensils from the previous night – first by the water in the nearby pond and then in water that we have stored in the house. Then I broom the house and throw away the garbage," she said.

It doesn't end there – Srikumari doesn't have even a minute to rest. "Even if I have a high fever, I have to work. I have no option," she said. In the past, she scavenged coal from nearby abandoned mines and sold it in town. When we met her, because of her illness, Srikumari was not able to work far from her house. Now, instead of coal scavenging, she has started raising livestock. She raises pigs, ducks and a few chickens. Protecting them from dogs and vultures comprises much of her day's work.

Suresh and Srikumari told us that even at night, they don't get any rest. "It's very hot inside the house because of the underground fires. Even with the fan running, we have a hard time sleeping," Srikumari whispered. Suresh added, "The area is so smoky and polluted. It takes a few hours before I get some sleep."

Living in the area has also become a bane for them socially. Suresh told us the story of an incident that happened to his family a few years ago. Three of his brothers also live in the *basti*. Together, they had arranged a marriage for his eldest brother's son. Arranged marriage is still a common practice amongst the majority of people in India. After the marriage was fixed, the bride's father – who lived in West Bengal – visited their *basti* to meet the elders of the family. The morning he arrived, after breakfast, Suresh took him to the lake for bathing. After that, the bride's father called off the marriage. "I took him to the *jordia* through the coal mine. He came back and said that his daughter will find it hard to stay here."

"You face so many problems living in the *basti*. What keeps you from moving to Belgoria?" Sandeep asked.

"There are no employment opportunities in the new place," Suresh replied. "Here we have employment, but we're slowly dying due to health issues. In Belgoria, without employment, we will quickly die due to hunger."

Poor people like Suresh know the importance of employment more than most others do. An emotional Suresh told us, "You won't understand what work means for people like me. If I don't work, I won't be able to live." Suresh only studied until the ninth grade. After that, he had to give up his studies and work. Srikumari never attended school.

Suresh did try to leave Jharia and find work elsewhere – once. In 1985, then in his early 20s, Suresh wasn't able to find work in Jharia for months. He travelled all around the area in search of work, even going to the neighbouring state of West Bengal. "The whole time I was unemployed, I couldn't even afford two square meals, as my father also had limited income. It was the hardest days of my life."

Finally, after trying for almost a year, he got work near Govindpur Road, which is now part of the state of Jharkhand. "I got a job working in a road construction company, and I was delighted," he said. "My two tasks were to lay stone chips and clean the newly constructed roads. But soon, I realized that I had been made a bonded labourer," he told us, a shadow crossing his face.

Armed security men would stand behind Suresh and his co-workers while they worked, and make sure they didn't take even a second's break. Every day, Suresh started work at seven a.m. and had to work for almost 15 hours. "We were beaten up if we asked for breaks," Suresh said. If any of the workers missed even a day's work, the owner would cut days of their salary. A horrified Suresh said, "I worked there for a week, but I didn't like it at all. I somehow escaped and returned to the *basti*."

After years searching for fixed employment, Suresh finally got another job in the coal industry in 1993, as a truck loader. Suresh looked at both of us and said, "You won't understand what unemployment and hunger means. If I move to Belgoria in the current conditions, I'll face both."

Srikumari, who was sitting next to Suresh, interrupted him. "Anyway, the government hasn't given us anything so far," she said with fire in her voice. "JRDA is supposed to make houses in Belgoria and Nipania. Belgoria is full and there are no places left. We've only been surveyed but not offered any cards." This is the case for the majority of people in this *basti*. "On top of it," added Srikumari, "we've been verbally threatened to leave the *basti*."

Sandeep asked the couple what they imagine life would be like if they move to Belgoria. Suresh told us that some of his friends who moved to Belgoria come back to the coal mines for work. "Some of my friends walk for many kilometres each side, to come to work and go back home. It's so far away. If I move there, I'll spend more than three hours every day commuting for work."

Srikumari is worried that shifting to Belgoria will mean that she'll have to live far away from her family and friends. Despite the terrible conditions, Suresh and Srikumari love aspects of the *basti* – they've grown up in the area, and lived closely with their relatives and friends for decades. Srikumari told us, "Our entire community lives here. We share our happiness and sadness with them and celebrate all the festivals together. If we move to Belgoria, all this community structure will be destroyed." There is also a fear that the JRDA will randomly shift people to Belgoria without thinking about family structure. "Many families have been broken. Brothers who have been living together are now forced to live separately," said Suresh.

He doesn't remember where he was born, but from the time he can remember, he has lived in the *basti*. Suresh and Srikumari were married when they were 2 years old, but she moved to Suresh's house when she was 15. Traditionally, in some parts of Indian society, child marriages are still prevalent, and people marry their kids at a very young age. However, the bride only moves in with the husband's family when the girl is older, after a *Gawna* ceremony takes places. This ceremony is associated with child marriage and marks the time when the bride moves in and the marriage is consummated. "We have special memories attached to this *basti*. I still remember the first day I came here. I was so shy," recalls Srikumari.

They have a particular affection for the place because Suresh's father and grandfather also lived and died in the *basti*. Suresh is a third-generation coal worker. His grandfather was born in another area and migrated to Jharia in search of work. He got work in the coal mines under a private contractor. Suresh's father was born in Jharia and also worked in the coal mines, along with his mother. Describing the history of his family, Suresh said, "Before the nationalization of coal, my parents used to work in underground coal mines for private contractors. After working for a few years in underground mines, they got jobs under another contractor, picking stone." After nationalization, Suresh's father got a job with BCCL doing loading and unloading work.

"We have been dependent on the coal industry for generations now. But now this very coal has become a curse for us," explained Suresh. "While the fires have terrible health impacts, we can't leave the area – we are completely dependent on it for survival. In fact, everyone in this *basti* is dependent on the coal industry for their basic survival." Standing suddenly, Suresh told us he wanted to take us around the village and explain why people didn't want to, or couldn't, move.

Near the pond, we noticed a group of children and a pregnant woman sitting on a wicker bench under a small lean-to structure that provided some shade. Suresh motioned us over to speak with them. The woman, about six months pregnant, wore a green and yellow saree. Her feet were bare and dirty, with gold-painted toenails. She looked tired. She told us her name is Titri Devi, 30 years old. As more and more children gathered around us – perhaps 20 or 30 – she told us that the fires in the village make everything incredibly hot. With a fan it's bearable, but with no fan it's hard to stand. She really feels the heat and dust from the mines, and it's very difficult to have little water. She's here because her husband works in the coal industry. Suresh told us that because of the pollution, people suffer from health problems such as fevers and breathing problems, but the government hospital is too far away. They usually go to the *basti* doctor, a local man with little formal training.

Suresh motioned for us to follow him. We walked through the village, stepping over three small pigs that lay in a crack in the road, tail to snout. As we walked further through the village, burning piles of coal on either side of the path clouded the air with smoke. A blackened and leafless tree stood to the right of the path. "Do you see that tree?" Suresh asked. "There's a fire below it and the gas caused the tree to die." It didn't take long to walk out of the main part of the village into an open area. The ground on one side of the path had caved in. "The land subsided there not long ago," said Suresh, pointing.

At the end of the path was a small house, an expanse of dirt ringed with coal fires, and then a huge, blackened and barren landscape dropping off into nothingness. We'd reached the end of the village – and the start of a huge open-cast mine. "Below us there's so much fire, if someone removed the first few layers of sand, we'd all be burnt in a second," Suresh said. We reached the edge and looked out past the coal fires.

At the edge of the village, a huge area had been excavated and giant piles of overburden ringed the hole. Active mining was going on below, and trucks moved up and down blackened paths into the dark pit. Red fires belched smoke on either side of the truck paths. Suresh told us that the village predates the mine, and at first people protested when the company opened that particular open-cast mine so close to their houses. Then the company gave 25 or 30 people employment to pacify them. However, the people soon realized the company wouldn't actually give them work – they just paid them a little money every month to keep them quiet.

Suresh introduced us to the man living in the house next to the mine, who was sitting outside the house and shaving another man. Wrapping up his work, he introduced himself as Dananjee Sharma, 25 years old – the village barber. A short, thin man with a black bowl cut, Dananjee wore only a short green lungi. Suresh and Dananjee alternated telling us that 15 to 20 days back, there was land subsidence in his house. "Where were you when the subsidence happened?" Savannah asked. Dananjee paused. He told us that he had been inside the house. Ushering us into that same house, he told us that he was stuck in the floor of the bedroom after the land subsided and the floor cracked. He stayed, screaming, for ten minutes until someone came to rescue him. He took us in to show us the damage. The walls of the bedroom were cracked, letting in the light and dust from outside. There were deep cracks in the bedroom floor. Suresh said that this isn't the first time land has subsided, but it is the first time anyone has been inside a house when it happened.

We asked Dananjee if he would like to move to Belgoria. "Can't you also shave people there?" Sandeep asked.

Dananjee shook his head. "How can I shave there if no one has any money? Why will they come?" He told us he also hasn't received a card from the survey that would allow him to get a flat in Belgoria.

As we exited the house, Suresh pointed to an area of dirt nearby. "The government mining company, BCCL, came here recently," he said. "They put a board here two days back saying that this is a fire zone and people shouldn't stay here. Then they took photos of the board, removed it, and left."

We crossed several low-built earth houses and dirty roads filled with garbage. As we walked, we passed several cracks in the ground where smoke was billowing out. Reaching a hut, Suresh called out "Mangli!" We waited for a few minutes, not sure who was coming. Slowly, 25-year-old Mangli Bhuiyan emerged from the hut. She was short, around five feet tall, wearing a green kurta (a long top) and pants. Her entire face was swollen – the left side more than the right. She held a scarf to her chin using both hands, and every now and then wiped her face with it. Suresh looked at her, and then looked at us and asked, "Why do you think she isn't moving to Belgoria?"

Mangli started to speak. "I have a hard time walking. I faint often and have a hard time breathing," she said, leaning on the mud hut. She was shivering as she talked to us. Her voice was low and we bent forward to hear her.

"She is suffering here, but at least she gets to eat," Suresh said. "If she moves to Belgoria, you wouldn't see Mangli. She would die of malnourishment and hunger."

A group of people had gathered around us. Suresh introduced us to 20-year-old Santosh Bhuiyan, Mangli's first cousin.

Suresh told him to come forward and tell us why he doesn't want to go to Belgoria. Santosh was very thin – both his body and his legs. His eyes were yellow, and he looked very sick. "It's unbearable here. But when I'm not sick, I get some work," he said, coughing. "My friends who have moved to Belgoria never get any work. I don't want to go there." He told us that he had a high fever and had been ill often in the last few months.

We understood what Suresh was explaining to us. He was showing us that although the people of the *basti* are suffering, they can't leave. Despite the curse coal has become for them, they are dependent on it for their livelihoods.

"Do you feel hopeful about the future?" Savannah asked.

Suresh nodded vigorously. "We have hope. If we all fight together, we'll get a better place to live and work, and our lives will improve."

Suresh asked us if we'd like to see some of the larger fires nearby and then drop him off at work. He and another man he introduced as Kundan Paswan piled into the car with us. We drove around the circumference of the open-cast mine, stopping to take some pictures of the red coal fires glowing and smoking in its base. On the other side of the mine, we drove for one or two minutes more and stopped. Getting out, we could see another *basti* to our left, with about 30 large fires right next to it. In front of us was a huge, glowing fire in a metre-wide crater. We walked across an area pocked with cracks and small fires to reach the large, fiery pit.

"What would you do right now if the ground subsided and we all fell in and died?" Parwaz asked Amit, laughing. Sandeep and Savannah laughed nervously.

"*Bhaiya* – brother, this is the most dangerous drive I've ever done," Amit said.

As we went to look more closely at the fire, Kundan told us that people have jumped into the burning hot crater to commit suicide. As we moved back from the fire, Savannah asked Kundan what one thing he thinks could really help Jharia. He hesitated for a minute, and looked at the ground. "One thing," he said, "is just give the people of Jharia basic human rights. To clean air, and water. To work. And to have good working hours." We all fell silent, thinking about his simple request for the people of Jharia. So basic, yet seemingly so unattainable.

Our visit to Golakd *basti* marked the end of our time in Jharkhand. Speaking to people in the state's coal mining areas had helped us realize that although coal mining affects the environment and people's health in places like Jharia, many people are fully dependent on this industry for their livelihoods. We wondered if the situation was similar or different in the Canadian oil sands, where we were heading next.

*Part III*

———

# JOURNEY TO ALBERTA

## Chapter Six

# A BLACK GOLD RUSH TOWN

*Within 20 kilometres of Fort McKay, there is development in every single direction of a community where people are living, and they are basically now in an industrial zone.*
— Karla Buffalo, Senior Manager of Government Relations, Fort McKay First Nation

Our taxi driver rolled down the window of the van and pointed to his left. "All this area used to be houses – now it's all gone," he said, shaking his head. We followed the line of his finger to a valley directly next to the highway. The neighbourhood there was completely destroyed. Lines of what used to be houses lay in square plots of white, ashy rubble. Blackened, burned-out husks of trucks sat in driveways. The whole area was surrounded by an orange fence, and the road going down into the settlement was barricaded by security personnel and police.

We'd just arrived in Fort McMurray, a northeastern Alberta town that is the beating heart of Canadian oil sands extraction. The town had faced its share of disasters in the past two years. In May 2016, a few months before we came to Fort McMurray, a massive wildfire broke out in the area. The town was evacuated May 3, just two days after fire was first spotted southwest of the city. The town's more than 80,000 residents were forced to flee, marking the largest wildfire evacuation in Canada's history.[54] The fire spread throughout northern Alberta and across the border into the neighbouring province of Saskatchewan before it was finally declared under control on July 4. The fire was big, and it was hungry. It consumed 2,400 structures and

6000 square kilometres of forest – an area a little bit larger than the entire province of Prince Edward Island, Canada, and about four times the size of the city of London, England.

The authorities got the fire under control only about 20 days before we arrived in Fort McMurray. When we first heard news of the fire, we were horrified by the situation and weren't sure whether we'd be able to go to Fort McMurray to do our research for this book. The news was full of pictures of the inferno looming over Fort McMurray, and a Canadian scientist we consulted told us to put down our pens and give up. "You might not be understanding the immensity of the situation. Fort Mac is evacuated, much of the city is burnt to the ground," he wrote. After getting his email, we'd looked at each other and wondered whether the Fort McMurray chapter was finished before we'd even started.

Many attributed the severity of this fire to Alberta's unusually dry El Niño winter and warm spring, as well as forest management practices in the area that had left large tracts of land ripe for fire.[55] Although some were quick to point the finger at climate change, leading scientists working in this area, such as Mike Flannigan, a professor of wildland fire from the University of Alberta, told the media that it was not possible to say that climate change caused this specific fire. However, Mike also stated that total Canadian wildfire activity – and the total area destroyed by fire – has been increasing in the past few years, and this is linked to climate change.[56] Our taxi driver (who preferred not to be named in this book) told us that while there's always a fire somewhere near town in the summer, it had always stayed in the bush – until now. "It just burnt like crazy," he told us. "It was too dry."

Later that day, we left our hotel on the fringes of Fort McMurray and walked to the city centre. On one side of the road were big box supermarkets bordered by strip malls, and on the other, small residential areas. A thin stream of traffic, mainly large trucks, moved down Franklin Avenue, Fort McMurray's main street. "This is a truck town!" said Sandeep, and laughed. "I've never seen such huge trucks in my life." The sidewalks were empty and the town was quiet. The hills on either side of the town were covered with trees, giving a glimpse of what the area would have looked like before oil sands development took off. Here and there, the forest ended abruptly in burnt, blackened patches.

Oil sands are exactly what they sound like – a natural mix of sand; clay or other minerals; water; and a viscous, heavy oil called bitumen.[57] And Alberta's oil sands, commercially developed since the 1960s, are huge. Alberta's oil reserves are an estimated 166 billion barrels – the third-largest oil reserves in the world, after Saudi Arabia and Venezuela.[58]

There are two ways to mine in the oil sands – open-pit and in-situ. In open-pit mining, sand is scooped up from the surface using huge shovels that load it into trucks, which take the sand to another facility, where hot water and chemicals are used to separate the sand from the bitumen. The separation process produces waste by-products: a wet mixture of sand, water, fine clays, residual bitumen and many types of toxic compounds, which are stored in open ponds called tailings ponds. In in-situ mining, which is used for areas where the bitumen is too deep to be dug up from the surface, high-pressure steam is pumped underground to loosen the bitumen found there, and then the heated and less viscous bitumen is pumped up to the surface. Open-pit mining can access about 20 per cent of the recoverable barrels in the oil sands, and in-situ can access the other 80 per cent.[59] While there are three oil sands areas in northern Alberta, only the Athabasca oil sands, where Fort McMurray is located, has deposits close enough to the surface to be mined through open-pit methods. Altogether, through a combination of open-pit and in-situ mining, 2.3 million barrels of oil were produced every day in 2014.[60]

Governments, companies and individuals have all benefitted economically from this black gold rush. Until recently. A 2016 paper on the oil sands from the Oxford Institute for

Energy Studies reported that in early 2015, profits from the oil sands made up about 5 per cent of Canada's GDP – although this number was predicted to drop further alongside crude prices.[61] Canada is a major crude oil exporter. It exports roughly 75 per cent of its total production – 97 per cent of that to the US, and 3 per cent to Asia and Europe.[62] The oil sands industry also made the fortunes of hundreds of thousands of workers from all over Canada. And it made the town of Fort McMurray. Like in India's coal belt, most people living in the town work either directly in the industry or in supporting industries, such as restaurants and shops.

Fort McMurray, called Fort McMoney by some, used to be the place where a tradesperson in their 20s could make a starting salary of over C$100,000 a year (about US$75,000).[63] Earlier that day, as we passed rows of blackened trees by the side of the highway, our taxi driver told us that Fort McMurray was where people came to make it big and get rich. "Two years ago, it was easy to get a job. And any normal job, you can make like $100,000 (about US$75,000) a year. I used to drive a UPS truck, and I used to make a hundred grand a year, with a regular driving licence," he said. A Statistics Canada survey from 2011 reported that the highest Canadian incomes – a median family income of C$186,782 (about US$140,000) – were found in the oil sands area around Fort McMurray. The driver told us that times have changed. "Now it's a really tough time."[64]

Apart from raking in cash that most Canadians in their 20s could only dream of, most workers were living a relatively luxurious life on the job site. Many didn't live in Fort McMurray, but were "fly in, fly out" workers, travelling to the area where they worked for one- or two-week shifts, and spending the same amount of time at home. During their working week, they would be stationed at camps near their oil sands work sites. According to Jay Bueckert, the Fort McMurray regional director of the Christian Labour Association of Canada, which primarily represents construction and maintenance workers in the oil sands, going to these camps "is like going into a Best Western or any kind of four-star resort. The quality of the camps has substantially improved over the last 15 years. You talk to our members, and they will say it's all the comforts of home plus they supply all your food." He told us that the camps provide everything from yoga classes to CrossFit instructors, and organize sports leagues. Mount Logan Lodge, a work camp run by Suncor near their new Fort Hills mine, 90 kilometres north of Fort McMurray, advertises rooms with double beds and private bathrooms, dining rooms serving everything from Italian to Asian food, and amenities like a movie theatre, golf simulator, indoor hockey rink, baseball diamond and soccer pitch.

When we interviewed Ken Smith, an oil sands worker and the president of the union Unifor Local 707-A, we asked him whether oil sands workers face any health issues from their work and daily lives in the area. "I come from the underground mining industry," he said. "Health impacts on underground miners, like coal miners, are much higher than the oil sands industry. We do have some silica dust, but it is very low or minimal in this area. There are other toxins from the oil industry, but they are monitored constantly," he said. "Companies do a better job today compared to what they did 10 years ago or 20 years ago. The companies want healthy employees and not sick employees."

Boom had turned to bust by the time we arrived in Fort McMurray – which, along with the wildfire, explained the quiet streets. As oil prices began to drop in 2014, sliding from US$115 a barrel in June 2014 to a low of approximately US$27 in January 2016, there was a cascade of effects in the oil sands. By the time we reached Fort McMurray, many oil sands workers had lost their jobs – an estimated total of 44,000 jobs since the downturn started in 2014.[65]

These job losses impacted individuals as well as the provincial coffers. Many workers in Fort McMurray could no longer afford the mortgages on their houses and simply left town, mailing their keys to the bank. The psychological pressure on laid-off workers and their communities was huge. In the first half of 2015, Alberta's suicide rate climbed by 30 per cent, which some connected to the oil sands layoffs and poor state of the economy.[66] By August 2016, the drop in oil prices, compounded by the millions of dollars the government spent combatting the expensive Fort McMurray wildfire, sent the Province of Alberta spiralling into debt.[67] In the following months, prices of oil recovered a little, yet Alberta's economy was slow to rebound. Rachel Notley, the premier of the province, stated in October 2016 that it would be "premature" to say the worst was behind the province.[68]

The fallout from the slump in the oil sands industry underlines how much Alberta, and by association Canada, depends on it for jobs and revenue. It also highlights how important it is to plan effectively for a transition for this sector as the world moves towards renewables. Many would agree that the faster we move away from oil sands extraction, the better.

The oil sands have a destructive impact on the environment. Oil sands oil is dirtier than conventional oil. The Oxford Institute for Energy Studies 2016 report states that despite producers' efforts to limit environmental impacts, "Oil sands production still creates more land disturbance, uses more water, and emits more greenhouse gases per barrel produced than conventional production of light oil."[69] Natural Resources Canada reports that the oil sands account for 9.3 per cent of Canada's greenhouse gas emissions, while Canada's emissions make up 1.6 per cent of the world's total emissions.[70] That means the oil sands are producing more greenhouse gas emissions than many small countries, such as Sweden.[71]

Bitumen extraction and upgrading also causes regional air pollution and puts pressure on water resources. The same Oxford report states that current mining production (excluding planned new projects) requires two million barrels of water per day from Alberta's Athabasca River, and withdrawals could triple by 2030 if production grows as estimated. Both open-pit and in-situ extraction causes land disturbance. And after companies are done mining, it takes a long time to clean up the mess – including the tailings ponds. Less than 1 per cent of land disturbed by oil sands mining to date has been certified reclaimed. Finally, and importantly, impacts on human health from the oil sands are also a matter of great concern, instigating a battle of reports and experts in recent years.[72]

◆

Many people and communities in and around Fort McMurray are economically dependent on the oil sands. This means that there's some support for industry, while at the same time there's a great deal of opposition due to the industry's negative impacts.

We realized this when we visited Fort McKay, a small community about 60 kilometres north of Fort McMurray, on the bank of the Athabasca River and smack in the middle of the major oil sands extraction operations. The community is surrounded by 17 oil sands mines and in-situ projects, ten more proposed projects and numerous existing and proposed pipelines. Fort McKay is home to about 800 people, predominantly from the Fort McKay First Nation (FMFN) and the Fort McKay Métis Community. The town represents a paradox. Fort McKay has experienced significant health and environmental impacts from industry activity, which we learned when we visited the community. Yet the FMFN is one of Alberta's First Nations working most closely with, and benefitting from, the industry – their chief, Jim Boucher, suggested in 2016 that the time might be right for Fort McKay to start a First Nations–owned and controlled oil sands project, and agreed that same year to invest C$350 (about US$260) million for a one-third stake in a new Suncor tank farm facility.[73]

The FMFN owns ten companies that provide services, such as construction, to the oil sands industry. From 2011 to 2015, these companies paid out C$200 million (about US$150 million) annually in salary and wages to staff in Alberta. In its annual report, the First Nation rates industry partners in three categories – exceptional, valued and aspiring – to "demonstrate the potential and possibility of stronger working relationships with FMFN and to highlight where improvements can be made." For instance, Suncor, Canadian Natural and Syncrude are "exceptional" partners.[74]

As we drove into Fort McKay, we saw a town of a few buildings spaced out along a paved, dusty road. Bungalows lined residential streets just off the main road. The town was quiet, with only a few construction workers and dogs out at 11 a.m. There were few signs of wealth, one of which was the Dorothy McDonald Business Centre, a large, new-looking lodge with big glass windows and an expansive parking lot. We parked there and walked towards the Fort McKay Sustainability Department office, housed in a white trailer on the hill.

"Is this the sustainability office?" we asked a young woman with a short black bob standing outside the trailer. "Nope – you're on the wrong reserve!" she joked, and then motioned us inside. The receptionist ushered us into an expansive boardroom with a long brown wood table and a smart board.

We met two Elders inside – Peter, a friendly, soft-spoken man with a silver brush cut and glasses, and Harvey, whose face was creased with laugh lines and who was wearing dark pants, a casual shirt and a black ball cap. As we sat down at the table, Peter told us that he was born and brought up in Fort McKay, while Harvey told us he was born out on the trapline – an area of land where a member of his family had rights to trap and had built a cabin. After we explained our research about a transition in Alberta away from fossil fuels and the oil sands towards renewable energy, Peter chuckled and said, "Well it's got to come to an end sometime."

Leaning back in her chair, Savannah asked, "How have the oil sands affected the environment in Fort McKay?"

Both men were silent for a moment and looked across the table at each other. Peter sighed and said, simply, "It's damaged it."

Oil sands development first took off in the 1960s in the area around Fort McKay. Harvey told us that since the industry came to Fort McKay, "Everything, everything has changed here. It's all different. The oil sands changed the whole thing. Changed the place. Nothing's normal like before." He told us that it isn't possible to hunt and gather food around the town anymore because "they destroyed everything. Fish are no good in the river. Berries are no good." Peter added that you have to go further to find wild game, and the moose meat tastes strange – not like it used to. Before coming to Fort McKay we had read about these issues with wild foods, and about the community's health problems.

"Are there health impacts on community members from the oil sands?" Sandeep asked.

Harvey sat up straight and quipped, "Nobody's healthy around here – except me, I guess!" and we all laughed. The conversation turned more sombre when Peter replied, "There's more cancer. From the pollution, I guess. Air pollution, water pollution. From industry. I've been lucky not to get sick." We had smelled a strong chemical odour when driving into town, and asked them to tell us about the air. "You've got to be tough to live here!" Harvey exclaimed. "The air will kill you in no time. We're right in the middle of the oil sands."

These worrisome environmental and health impacts had also come up during a conversation we had with Alvaro Pinto, the Fort McKay First Nation director of sustainability, and Karla Buffalo, senior manager of government relations, in the same boardroom shortly before we met Peter and Harvey.

Alvaro and Karla described Fort McKay as a community surrounded by the oil sands on all sides and making the best of a difficult situation. Karla told us that prior to 2012, there was no land use plan for the area. Development was approved project by project without a broader understanding of how it was going to affect the landscape. This led to a situation where today, according to Karla, "within 20 kilometres of Fort McKay, there is development in every single direction of a community where people are living, and they are basically now in an industrial zone." Karla told us that although the situation has improved due to a land use plan, development is still approved project by project instead of according to some type of master plan. And there is no consideration of how much total development can occur on the landscape without causing a serious imbalance in the environment.

Savannah asked Karla and Alvaro whether any health study had been conducted connecting environmental impacts to community members' health. Alvaro sighed and shook his head. He said that they had wanted to do such a study for years and were working towards it, but were still far from the type of comprehensive, long-term health study needed. Such a study would be very expensive and required expertise they didn't possess in the community, so Fort McKay was trying to partner with government, universities and industry to find the resources. The lack of a long-term health study reminded us of Jharia, where we'd been only a short time before.

However, even without such a study, the evidence of environmental harm in Fort McKay is clear. "There is noise, water pollution, air pollution, odour issues," Alvaro said. "There are impacts on wildlife. It's scarce now, so people have to go further away to hunt – 20 kilometres, 30 kilometres. And people don't fish on the Athabasca River anymore."

In Fort McMurray, we interviewed Terry Abel, executive vice-president of the Canadian Association of Petroleum Producers (CAPP), a lobby group representing the oil sands industry. Abel had different views about monitoring. "You will probably not find a more heavily monitored industry in the world," he said. "The industry spends in excess of $200 million a year to monitor their impact." He told us that there are numerous and ongoing studies about the health of people and the environment in the region, but none of these studies point to any direct link between the health of communities or workers and the result of producing oil sands. Nonetheless, studies and monitoring are ongoing.

Irrespective of what's been concluded from monitoring so far, it's clear that air quality is one of the biggest concerns in Fort McKay – and one of the areas where considerable monitoring is taking place. Alvaro told us during our conversation that they "see a lot of things coming through the air emissions." He told us that Fort McKay has its own specialized air monitoring station in partnership with Environment Canada. Which is important – because issues arise.

In June 2016, a few months before our visit, Canadian Natural Resources Limited, a nearby oil sands operator, was fined C$500,000 (about US$370,000) for two separate leaks of poisonous hydrogen sulphide gas that occurred in 2010 and 2012. Hydrogen sulphide smells like rotten eggs and is poisonous and explosive. The company had failed to report one of the leaks for up to a month, and the Alberta government only started investigating when it received complaints from residents of Fort McKay and high readings from air monitoring stations in the region.[75]

The community has been calling for an assessment of the cumulative effects of air pollution for years – not just of these acute events but also of everyday exposure. A report by the Alberta government and the provincial energy regulator, released in September 2016, suggested that, at least some of the time, Fort McKay air contains potentially harmful levels of chemicals including hydrogen sulphide, a toxin, and benzene, a carcinogen. The report stated that there is potential that ongoing exposure to certain substances found in the air could impact human health, yet "it is not clear what the implications are to human health, and further assessment is necessary."[76] The report has spurred further ongoing research.[77]

In the boardroom, Karla leaned forward in her chair. She told us that it's not just health and environmental impacts the community is facing. "Some of the other impacts when you think about health are stress impacts in the community," she said. "There are ongoing daily odours and air pollution in this community – we regularly have to call in odour complaints that tend to be unaddressed." She told us that there are also concerns about quality and quantity of water, as well as whether animals, plants and fruits harvested from the area are healthy. "All of that causes kind of a constant stress." There's also stress because of the potential for impacts to the environment. "If there is a breach in the tailings pond, if there is an explosion at one of the plants, if there is a fire at one of the plants – all of that can have direct impacts here in the community that provide a lot of risk, so community members kind of have to live with that."

"Another component really important to understand in terms of health is cultural impacts," Karla told us. She said that lifestyle has changed a lot in the community in the last 30 to 40 years. "This was once a very traditional community, where most people relied on hunting and game for their diet, and it was a very isolated community that had more traditional roles." She told us that now people have to plan for when they're able to go out on the land. "Because they're on shift work, they can't be as spontaneous as before," she said. "The routes on the landscape change quite a bit in terms of access," she added. "The routes can change quite a bit without notice. We've got community members that have been trapped in between mines because gates have been locked, or you've got security personnel that won't let you through a gate that's supposed to be open, and so the way that people have traditionally been able to be on the land has been impacted." She sighed and said, "This affects your ability to transfer knowledge, by being able to be active on the landscape, by taking your kids out and having the same experience that you did as a child with your grandparents..." She continued, "When you have knowledge transmission that isn't happening anymore, you lose traditional knowledge, you lose language and sometimes you lose connectedness amongst families... that whole transition affects a community."

Despite these numerous and varied impacts, for most of the First Nations people living in Fort McKay, fleeing the industrial zone that their town has become is out of the question. The town, and the area surrounding it, is their traditional territory, to which they have a deep connection. Karla said, "It's not that you can replace the landscape and just go somewhere else to hunt and fish and trap and have the same experience. There is a connection to the land that provides a level of health and spirituality that cannot be transferred over without loss."

She explained that for a family that's been on a territory for hundreds and hundreds of years and is very familiar with that territory – what it provides, how to navigate it, changes in the environment over time, the history of who was birthed there, married there – all those types of stories have a spiritual connection and a physical connection that is important to health and well-being. When interruption happens – for example, a mine is built over an area where a family used to do all their practice – that changes a person's ability to have connection to land, and connection to culture.

Our conversation with Karla raised some questions for both of us. Given these impacts from living in the heart of the oil sands, how did Fort McKay reconcile having such significant business interests in the industry?

"Jim, the chief, is a visionary," Alvaro told us. He explained that Jim Boucher first started out as chief by pushing for change in how the community dealt with industry. "In the past, there was a lot of pushback from this community towards industry. Jim realized that instead of fighting something that is going to be inevitable, maybe we should try to be part of the process, but in a way that we still try to protect the community, the environment and our interests."

Today, FMFN owns and operates ten companies. In addition, private entrepreneurs in the community own 19 businesses, many of which offer construction and other services to the oil sands. According to Alvaro, a few of them have been so successful they've become millionaires. "The individual owners of the private companies deal directly with the oil companies," Alvaro said. "They go through the bidding and procurement process. They have an advantage because the oil companies really try to accommodate the Aboriginal business owners. We also push for that when we are negotiating long-term agreements." As talk turned to employment, he added, "If any person in McKay wants a job, they can get it – either in oil companies or our companies."

The FMFN is supportive of economic development within Alberta and Canada but believes that if economic development is going to happen on traditional territory, there needs to be balance. "There needs to be direct participation by Fort McKay, influencing how that development is going to happen – environmental protections, agreements, standards that need to be put in place," Alvaro said. We asked Alvaro what would happen in the future if oil sands extraction ends.

"I think eventually the resource will be gone," he told us. "I think what McKay is considering is how to be part of the development as long as it can. Then they'll start considering what's the alternative."

Later on, still reflecting on this conversation, we asked Peter and Harvey what they thought. "Has all this development made people's lives better in any way?" Savannah asked.

"Well it's given people jobs," Peter said, leaning back in his chair.

"No," Harvey said firmly. "Before, things were better. People lived a long life. Had lots of exercise. The water was good." He crossed his arms.

We ask them both what they think should happen with oil sands development in this area. "Should the oil sands stop?" Savannah asked. "Or should they be developed in a different way?"

Harvey frowned. "There's no way it will stop – never," he said. "Oil sands companies pay a lot of money to government. They don't listen to Indians."

Peter nodded. "Right now everyone needs oil – I need gas in my car. But maybe there's a safer way to get it out – to get the gas and the oil out." We asked if they think an energy transition will ever come. Peter smiled. "Well it's got to. All those things – coal, oil – there'll be nothing left some day. I don't know where people will turn – probably solar. You could charge up your car with wind. But someday it will all be gone. It's got to be."

Later that evening, once we got back from Fort McKay, we went for a walk along the banks of the Athabasca River in Fort McMurray. Half-finished development projects, apparently abandoned, lined the road. "You know, the story of the oil sands isn't that different than the story of coal mining in India," Sandeep said. "Of course, the countries' contexts are different, but in both situations, many people are economically dependent on the resource, while an even larger number of people suffer because of the environmental and health impacts caused by extraction."

Savannah nodded. "That's true," she said. "And we need to move away from harmful processes like oil sands extraction and fossil fuels in general. But being here makes it clear we also need a plan, because we live in societies hooked on fossil fuels – for employment, and for every aspect of our daily lives." We walked silently for a moment. "And you know," Savannah said, "While Fort McMurray and Fort McKay are at the epicentre of the oil sands, the impacts from extraction have actually spread much further. Tomorrow I'm hoping we'll meet Robert, a friend of a friend who's also a trapper and an oil sands worker, who can tell us more."

# Chapter Seven

## THE TRAPPER, HUNTER AND MILLWRIGHT

*If the oil sands industry shuts down in the future, people here will have a hard time – they are so dependent on the oil industry, they won't have employment.*

—Raymond Ladouceur, Métis Elder and
resident of Fort Chipewyan

His 200-kilogram Ski-Doo was stuck in the ice. Seventeen at the time, he was out in the bush for his yearly hunting and trapping season in the traditional territory of the Mikisew Cree, a First Nation that resides in northern Alberta. Now in his 30s, he still recalls how he got himself to safety within half an hour. "I knew that I'd have no more than an hour. Because in one hour, I would lose all my energy, get hungry and collapse," said Robert Grandjambe, a fourth-generation trapper and hunter, and a member of the Mikisew Cree First Nation.

"I knew that there was no one around to help me – I was deep inside the forest. I pushed myself harder and somehow managed to lift the Ski-Doo back onto firmer ice," said Robert, a friendly, well-built man with brown eyes and short black hair. He motioned with his hands, showing how he struggled to lift the heavy Ski-Doo, a type of snowmobile used for travel in snowy areas.

We first met Robert in Fort McMurray. Wearing casual clothing, black sunglasses perched on his head, he offered to give us a tour of the oil sands operations around the town. After about five minutes on the road in his large black truck, we got onto a four-lane highway with huge trucks zooming by in both directions. The sides of the road were bordered by stands of burnt-down trees mixed with patches of spiky purple fireweed.

Robert knew Fort McMurray well because he works near the town as a millwright for 14 weeks every year, for different oil sands companies. His job as a millwright involves installing and repairing machinery. The rest of the year, he spends his time trapping and hunting in the wild boreal forests of northern Alberta.

"Ice conditions are really different now," Robert said. "When I started trapping and hunting as a kid, the ice used to be thicker and stronger during winters, and you could easily walk on it. Now the ice doesn't freeze the same way." Robert was 6 years old when he started helping his father set up their trapline.

Since then, he hasn't looked back and has spent 26 winters of his life on the trapline. "Now you can't trust the ice. It's sketchy," he added. Sandeep looked at Robert with interest from the passenger's seat, and Savannah leaned forward from the back. "It's becoming harder," he explained further. "This is how trappers will be eliminated slowly. There are a lot of transitions. There is rain in the middle of January. This was never before. So the situation is totally unexpected now. It's too hard for a trapper to go around in the middle of January with unexpected ice and wet rain."

"Do you think climate change has anything to do with it?" Savannah asked.

"Yeah, you can definitely see the difference in the entire ecosystem. This is all due to climate change," Robert replied, shaking his head. "Changing climate is a big challenge. As a trapper, I often have to fight against the government to protect my traditional rights, and deal with the conditions in the forest. But now changing climate is an extra challenge over and above other struggles. You work hard and deal with other challenges. But climate change is different – you have no control over it."

It was clear that Robert was attuned to the land and to the

changes that made his work as a trapper and hunter increasingly uncertain. Trappers like Robert have to be very close to nature and pay attention to small signs and subtle shifts that mark the changing of the seasons. They notice when geese are getting their nests ready, or when a beaver starts to replenish its food for the winter. This helps them determine when to prepare their trapline.

After a few moments of silence, Robert said, "Just ten years ago, the seasons would come and go and their timings were predictable. You knew when the snow was coming and the summer or the spring was on the way. As a hunter, you have to be prepared for firewood, food supplies and also to gather everything required to survive long durations of cold weather." He paused and said, "If I fast-forward to now, the weather conditions feel contradictory. Very contradictory to what I was taught as a kid."

Robert told us the rapidly changing weather conditions are hard for humans and animals alike. "Animals are also hurt while crossing the river because the river doesn't get very good ice quality when it freezes. They are becoming vulnerable to predators," he said. He told us several stories about the impact climate change is having on animals in the forest. For instance, muskrats build little nests called push-ups that provide shelter for them during winter. At first freeze, they clear a hole in the ice and pull up submerged water plants to create a hut. The hut freezes, and when snow falls on it, it creates a perfect, insulated shelter for the muskrat, with access to the water below. But if the snow doesn't fall, or isn't the same quality, the nests can freeze through and don't provide any shelter at all. "As a trapper, now, when I go and look for these push-ups, they are often frozen right through," he said.

Robert told us there are many such examples of how animals are being affected and the ecosystem is changing. The migratory path that bison have followed for hundreds of years is totally disturbed now. Each year, bison come to the Peace River after ice accumulates, and then cross and continue their migration. "Now, due to climate change, when they get to the Peace River, the river is still flowing. They are stuck, and their predators, like wolves, start eliminating them," Robert said. The result is that, now, bison come, encounter wolves and return back north.

As he was describing the effects of climate change on different animals, the scenery we drove through changed. In the distance, we saw a huge industrial site emanating large clouds of smoke into the atmosphere.

"Look at that smoke!" Sandeep said. "I'm amazed by the volume... the scale is similar to the coal fires in Jharia."

Robert laughed. "That's nothing," he said. "That's the oil sands site run by Suncor. That's only one of the chimneys emitting smoke. There are three of them, same magnitude. With full capacity it looks like something else!" The car windows were open, and we smelled a pungent odour. It was oppressive and strong.

"What is that smell?" Sandeep asked.

"It's the steam coming out of the extraction process. Bitumen is separated from sand using steam and other chemicals," Robert told us.

"Don't you feel annoyed about the smell?" said Sandeep.

"You have to deal with it," Robert said. "You have to deal with it to work there. It's not a healthy smell – I'm not working as a mint picker!" We laughed wryly, but it seemed sad.

We drove past the Suncor site. Robert told us that although he's able to deal with the smell, the air pollution caused by the oil sands disturbs the migratory paths of the birds that come to Alberta. "Many birds used to migrate and come to Fort Chipewyan before. Now the oil sands are here, so very few birds are going to Fort Chipewyan," he said.

Robert has traced the migratory birds from the United States border and followed them through their journey several times in the past. "Now migratory birds are taking different routes," he said. He told us that the birds don't come to areas around the oil sands operations, because of the air pollution.

A few minutes later, we saw a vast grey pond on one side of the road. Robert stopped the car and pulled over. The pond was surrounded by a tall barbed wire fence. Its surface was calm and flat, interrupted by a series of small bright orange scarecrows. We'd heard a lot about tailings ponds, but it was disconcerting to see one in person.

According to the Pembina Institute, a leading Canadian environmental think tank, tailings ponds currently cover more than 220 square kilometres of northern Alberta, amounting to one trillion litres of fluid tailings.[78] They contain toxic materials and emit air pollutants like greenhouse gases, volatile organic compounds, nitrous oxides and hydrogen sulphide. Cleanup methods for the ponds are currently still experimental.[79]

"Is this the tailings pond that was part of the big Syncrude lawsuit?" Savannah asked.

Robert shook his head. "Not this one, but it isn't far. The one where the ducks died. The leak came from internal sources – the guy who counted the ducks was my friend. He actually found about 1,600 dead ducks, but he was told not to tell that there were so many of them."

The case Robert was talking about is well known in Canada and garnered international media attention. In 2010, oil sands operator Syncrude was fined C$3 million (about US$2.25 million) – the largest environmental penalty to date in Alberta's history – for failing to prevent the death of 1,606 migratory ducks that landed on one of its tailings ponds near Fort McMurray in 2008.[80] Tailings ponds are an attractive resting spot for migratory birds because they are warm, but they are also deadly. In this case, the ducks died after landing on the tailings pond, getting coated in oil and sinking to the bottom.[81] Just days after Syncrude agreed to pay the $3-million penalty in the first case, it happened again. Despite increased attempts by the company to deter birds, 230 ducks died after landing in another Syncrude pond.[82]

Tailings ponds don't just kill ducks – there is evidence they may leak. Suspicions about leaking tailings ponds were bolstered in 2014, when a study by Environment Canada found evidence strongly suggesting toxic tailings pond water is leaking, first leaching into groundwater and then seeping into the Athabasca River.[83]

When we interviewed Terry Abel of CAPP, we asked him about the tailings ponds. "There's lots of discussion and misunderstanding about the tailings ponds," he said. "It's important to understand that most of what exists in those tailings ponds is what exists in the natural environment already." He continued, "It's monitored heavily, and to date none of the studies can actually show that what you do detect in the river is necessarily from a tailings pond or from an industrial operation."

We drove past the Syncrude site. Rows of buildings in the front of the site partially covered a tangle of tall metal structures, some belching smoke. Beside it was a vast, barren grey-and-black landscape.

On the drive home, we spoke with Robert about his life as a trapper and a millwright. Robert wears two hats – he makes his income from the oil sands in one of his jobs, and from trapping and hunting in the other. He described his year. "Every year, I go out on the land in the first week of November and go on till the end of December. I come back in December, as I have to prepare and send my fur to Finland by the end of January. Then I go back to the bush and prepare to send furs for the next sale date at the end of February," he said.

"When you start in November, you don't come back for the next six weeks?" Sandeep asked.

Robert smiled. "I don't feel like coming back. My life is wonderful out there." In the bush, his day starts at six a.m. with some coffee after he lights a fire. Then he has breakfast and packs lunch. At seven a.m., he sets out on his Ski-Doo and starts checking the traps that he has laid for the animals. He walks a lot during the day – almost 12 kilometres out and then back. By the time he gets back to his cabin with the Ski-Doo, it's pitch dark and very cold, because it's been minus-20 degrees Celsius all day. He brings the fur in and cooks some dinner. He tells us he has to plan everything carefully, making sure he has enough gas and wood.

He spends all day amidst nature. "It's very peaceful. It's very fulfilling. You don't see people anywhere. You see wildlife, owls, and it's fascinating. It is so hard to put it in words. The brisk air, the cleanliness, the comfort of being able to feel healthy."

As we became immersed in his stories from the forest, he said, "Compare this to my life in Fort McMurray. I'm here in Fort McMurray to make money, that's all."

When he's in Fort McMurray, he gets up at four a.m. He packs his bag along with the food that he prepared the previous night. By six a.m., he's ready to hop onto the oil sands company bus, which takes an hour to reach the site, where his supervisor assigns him work. "Once the job is underway, it's intense and my day goes off pretty fast. We get some food and coffee breaks. After ten hours, my shift ends and I go back home in the same bus. My day is almost gone."

As we're about to say goodbye, Robert tells us, "Your story won't be complete if you don't visit Fort Chipewyan. If you go there, you'll understand how people live. Many people are economically dependent on the oil sands, and people also have different ideas about how the oil sands are affecting their health and environment."

We came back that night after thanking Robert for sharing his knowledge and showing us the oil sands areas. Taking the cue from Robert, we decided we had to go to Fort Chipewyan.

◆

Two days later, as our air taxi lifted off from Fort McMurray, we took in the beautiful landscape of Alberta's boreal forests. "It's stunning!" Sandeep said from mid-plane, and Savannah nodded in agreement, stuffed in the back amidst the cargo.

After leaving the area around Fort McMurray, where the green forest was interspersed with patches of blackened, burnt-down trees, the view below changed. Below us stretched out swaths of pristine forest dotted with intermittent lakes, small and big. When the light hit the streams snaking through the forest, they shone like the sun itself. There were no humans in sight. We were awed by the beauty of the landscape, and every five seconds the word *amazing* flashed in our minds.

After a while, we saw contrast on the horizon. We began to see ugly patches of blackened earth. Before coming to Fort McMurray, we had read how oil sands extraction has devastated the landscape, but now we were witnessing it first-hand. We had seen it from the car with Robert, but it was different to take it all in from above – as though someone had cut and peeled the forest off the face of the earth, leaving behind a black-and-grey expanse. It reminded us of the devastated landscapes we'd seen in the coal mining areas of India.

The contrast between mine and forest was stark. On one side was the scarred earth, devoid of any greenery or beautiful waterways, and right next to the clean line of its boundary sat spectacular forests.

Soon after, the pilot announced we were about to reach the Peace–Athabasca Delta (PAD). One of the world's largest inland deltas, it forms at the confluence of the Peace, Athabasca and Birch rivers west of Lake Athabasca.

The delta is considered by many to be the heart of northern Alberta's vast Wood Buffalo National Park. Bigger than the Netherlands, Wood Buffalo National Park is the largest national park in Canada and the second largest in the world. Declared a World Heritage Site in 1983 by the United Nations Educational, Scientific and Cultural Organization (UNESCO), it contains two wetlands: the PAD, and a whooping crane nesting site, both of which have been declared Wetlands of International Importance under the Ramsar Convention.

According to UNESCO, the park contains some of North America's largest tracts of undisturbed grass and sedge meadows and is the home of the world's largest herd of wood bison, a threatened species. The vast boreal forest within the park provides habitat for many other species, including the only breeding habitat in the world for the endangered whooping crane.[84] It's estimated that up to a million geese, swans and ducks migrate through the delta in the spring and fall.[85] This important land has been occupied and used by Indigenous peoples as part of their traditional territories for thousands of years, for hunting, fishing, trapping and many other important activities that support their cultural, spiritual and physical continuity.

"I never thought researching the fossil fuel industry would take me to the most spectacular place on Earth. I've *never* seen a more beautiful place than this – it's Canada's paradise," Sandeep said.

The national park stretches out to the west of Fort Chipewyan. We had read and heard that the PAD within the park had changed dramatically over the past decades. Some say that the water quality has degraded, others say that the water level has decreased. Some place the blame squarely on oil sands extraction. Others say problems in the delta are due to a complex mix of hydro dams upstream on the Peace River in the neighbouring province of British Columbia, industrial pollution from the oil sands and climate change. We asked Robert this question in Fort McMurray. "I can't say for sure that oil sands are the only contributor for pollution or loss of water in the Peace-Athabasca Delta. As far as I know, there's no study saying that this water contamination is directly from the oil sands," he said.

This isolated community of about 1,200 people can be accessed during summer by a boat or plane and in the winter by a winter road. Established by the North West Company in 1788, Fort Chipewyan is one of the oldest European settlements in Alberta. It is more than 200 kilometres north of Fort McMurray and downstream from the oil sands. Its residents are predominantly members of the Athabasca Chipewyan and Mikisew Cree First Nations, and Métis.

The first person we met in Fort Chipewyan was 74-year-old Raymond Ladouceur, a Métis Elder who has lived off the land his whole life as a trapper and commercial fisherman. When we reached his small, beautiful house, Raymond, a tall, well-built man wearing a checked shirt with red suspenders and a ball cap settled above a lined, friendly face, greeted us whole-heartedly. We sat down with him on his front deck.

"Oil sands development is slowly killing our area," he said. "People depend on oil companies for their living. But when they will take away everything, there will be nothing left in our area. In the past, you could drink water from the river. Now you can't because of the pollution caused by the oil sands. There is also a lot of foam on the lake. My younger days had no foam. These oil companies are discharging all sorts of chemicals and garbage."

We asked him whether water contamination was affecting community members. "When I was young, nobody died of cancer," he replied. "Now many people are dying of cancer. First the pulp mills had huge impact. Now the oil sands have serious impacts. The Indians call it a bug with many legs – because it travels through your body."

We asked Raymond what he thought the future would hold for the community and the oil sands. "If the oil sands industry shuts down in the future, people here will have a hard time – they are so dependent on the oil industry, they won't have employment," he said. He did think people would be interested in working in many other sectors, including the renewable energy industry. "I think solar power is the best thing in the world. I think solar is the way forward. Even the wind power is good too – there's a lot of wind. People will surely be interested in working for the renewable energy industry."

The extent of industry impact on the environment and community health is contested. Community members like Raymond clearly express concern about the health and environmental impacts of industry. However, we remembered our earlier conversation with Terry Abel of CAPP, who said that despite the numerous and ongoing studies into the health of the environment and people in the region, no study had pointed to any direct link between the health of communities and workers and the oil sands, though industry was still looking and monitoring its impact.

However, many other voices have raised concerns. In 2006, Dr. John O'Connor, then the community's physician, raised an alarm about the unusually high number of cases of a rare bile duct cancer and other diseases such as lupus and renal failure in Fort Chipewyan. Although not much is known about the bile duct cancer, called cholangiocarcinoma, scientists suspect it is connected to industrial toxins in water such as polycyclic aromatic hydrocarbons, an industrial pollutant linked to oil sands extraction and processing. After Dr. John raised these issues, members of Health Canada and the Alberta Cancer Board tried to take away his licence to work in 2007, charging him before the Alberta College of Physicians and Surgeons with causing "undue alarm" about environmental pollution. He was eventually absolved of the charges in 2009, the same year the Alberta Cancer Board released a study that confirmed higher than expected cancer rates in Fort Chipewyan.[86]

However, the controversy raged on. A 2010 Royal Society of Canada Expert Panel report about the environmental and health impacts of Canada's oil sands industry, and an April 2014 report from the Alberta government, found there was no credible evidence to link oil sands operations and the cancer cases in Fort Chipewyan.[87] Then, in July 2014, another study was released that found a link between elevated cancer rates in Fort Chipewyan and oil sands pollution, this one conducted jointly between University of Manitoba researchers, the Athabasca Chipewyan First Nation and the Mikisew Cree First Nation.[88]

Melody Lepine, director of government and industry relations for the Mikisew Cree First Nation, felt frustrated with the lack of monitoring in the oil sands region. "In Fort Chip, the community is finding contaminants associated with removal of hydrocarbons, but is not able to prove it because of the lack of monitoring programs. There has been no broad-based health study in Fort Chip. Health Canada, Alberta Health, the community are all waiting for each other to start," she told us. Melody said that the Mikisew Cree First Nation started its own community-based monitoring program because it was frustrated with the current insufficient monitoring. The program, established in 2008, tracks both Indigenous knowledge indicators of ecosystem health, and water quality and animal health parameters based on Western science, conducting its own studies and participating in studies with universities such as the University of Manitoba study mentioned above.[89]

Whether and to what extent industrial development in the oil sands is contaminating the area upstream, including Wood Buffalo National Park and the PAD, has been a matter of dispute. According to leading Alberta scientist David Schindler, government and the oil sands industry claimed for years that pollution in the lower Athabasca River system stemmed from soil erosion, forest fires and other natural phenomena.[90] The Athabasca River flows north, so any pollution from the upstream oil sands could travel with it. However, despite a lack of adequate and coordinated monitoring, a number of studies have begun to make the impacts clearer. Scientists released research in 2009 and 2010 that challenged the government's and oil sands industry's claims. They found that the oil sands industry was releasing substantial amounts of polycyclic aromatic compounds and other pollutants into the Athabasca River and its watershed.[91] After a period of dispute, government expert panels supported these results, and also found that monitoring programs in the area were insufficient to determine the extent of the pollution.[92]

Other research continues to emerge, including a 2013 study showing that a much larger area has been contaminated with polycyclic aromatic compounds than previously thought – the compounds were found in lakes more than 90 kilometres from the bitumen upgraders producing them, and the levels were found to have increased over time as bitumen production increased.[93]

Research suggests that the oil sands may be affecting local food sources as well. A 2013 study by Environment Canada and Parks Canada scientists found that concentrations of mercury had substantially increased in some types of gull and tern eggs at Mamawi Lake, located in the PAD, with the oil sands industry the likely source (though it stated that more research was needed to confirm this).[94] Soon afterward, the Alberta government put out a consumption advisory about eating gull and tern eggs on Lake Athabasca and Mamawi Lake due to the dangerous mercury levels.[95] A 2007 report by Kevin Timoney, an ecologist at Treeline Ecological Research, found that a number of studies have reported fish with deformities in the Lake Athabasca area, while Indigenous people have also noted an increase in abnormalities. Oil sands contaminants have the potential to cause such abnormalities, but the report did not draw a conclusive link between oil sands development and the deformed fish. It did conclude that science and traditional ecological knowledge suggest "rates of fish abnormalities may be higher than expected, may be increasing, and may be related to changes in water quality."[96] Locals like Raymond expressed concern that pollution of the delta was polluting the fish. "The fish look different and deformed, the whitefish are getting skinny and dying," he said. He told us that people avoid eating the big fish that they know are polluted, but think small fish are still okay.

We remembered our conversation with Robert back in Fort McMurray. "For some years now, I see more than one deformed fish in every catch. You can see the hump in the back of the fish, damaged gills, and also cysts in them," he told us. "With the whitefish, you can see red marks around their gills. Now the trout have really skinny bodies and big heads – probably because of the lack of food. I'm not a scientist, but I know what good fish is and is not. So I throw away the bad ones and keep the good ones."

Savannah asked Robert if he thought oil sands pollution was causing these problems. "I don't know," he said. "I can't say whether it's the oil sands or not. I would just say I don't know."

Back in Fort Chipewyan, we were about to go out on the delta with Robert's dad, who has the same name as his son – Robert Grandjambe. He promised to take us out and show us what we had begun referring to as "the delta in environmental dispute."

We woke up early and waited for Robert Sr. outside our lodgings. He came in his truck, with a boat attached to the back. We knew it was him right away – he looked so much like his son. We greeted him, then wasted no time. Sandeep hopped into the back of the truck, Savannah into the front.

At the shore, we piled into his boat. As we set out on the water, the massive Lake Athabasca spread out in front of us. It looked huge, almost like an open ocean, with sparkling blue-grey water broken only by patches of treed islands. The sun was shining, reflecting brightly on the water. "It's heavenly out here!" said Sandeep. It was hard to imagine that this area was the subject of one of the most controversial environmental disputes in the region.

Robert Sr. had a different perspective on the community. He told us it was important to know that the community was very dependent on the oil sands industry for employment. "Everyone here works for the oil industry. Directly or indirectly. I'm also indirectly dependent on the oil industry – I have clients who work for the oil industry." He claimed that the people of Fort Chipewyan have made a lot of money from oil sands development.

It is true that the oil sands have presented economic opportunities for First Nations like the Mikisew Cree First Nation and the Athabasca Chipewyan First Nation. The Mikisew Cree First Nation owns approximately ten companies through the Mikisew Group of Companies, several of which provide various services to oil sands companies. The Athabasca Chipewyan First Nation has 18 businesses through Acden, its group of companies that provide services to the oil sands industry. In addition, many community members are employed in the industry. However, some community members have described it as making the best of a bad situation. "Forty years ago, it was trapping, and that livelihood was stripped, so now people are left trying to find other ways to put food on the table," Athabasca Chipewyan youth leader Mike Mercredi told CBC News in 2014.

Eriel Deranger, as Athabasca Chipewyan First Nation spokesperson, told the *Edmonton Sun* news website that she does not support an immediate shutdown of the oil sands. She said that the Athabasca Chipewyan First Nation owns companies active in the oil sands, but she supports discussing how to transition to renewable forms of energy without damaging the economy. "We recognize the economic opportunities the oil sands has brought us, but it's time for us to start talking about making a transition," she told the website. "We're not afraid to have those conversations."[97]

◆

Our experience in Fort Chipewyan left us with a lot to think about. Soon after we arrived back in Fort McMurray, we met Robert again. Sandeep had cooked Indian food for him before we left for Fort Chipewyan, using spices we'd brought from India. This time, Robert had offered to cook us moose that he'd hunted himself. As he prepared the moose, he told us that he was curious about our experience in Fort Chipewyan. He told us there was one topic we hadn't heard much about. "There is a complete breakdown of social structure within the community," he said.

Robert grew up in a community where people were close to one another. People would hunt and trap and bring food for other community members. Today, he said that doesn't happen. "Nobody socializes anymore. When the oil sands support a particular individual, then other community members feel left out.

This leads to a lot of animosity. There's competition for who gets work, employment. The money aspect has really played a huge role and is breaking down the social structure of the community culture. Now everyone is thinking, *What can I get?*"

Robert told us that hunting and trapping, traditional activities, are less popular today. "I know that the number of trappers has reduced. The fur industry was crushed in the 1980s, when the oil sands industry expanded in the region. Work in the oil sands also made working in the fur industry less attractive."

As we sat down to eat, Robert told us he was worried that as the oil sands continue to expand, these traditional practices of trapping and hunting will be destroyed. He wondered whether, someday, oil sands development will expand into Wood Buffalo National Park. "First Nations need to be smart," he said. "Now you see so many winter roads and bridges. Why are they building so many wide and big bridges and roads for wintertime? For a town of 1,200 people. This isn't for the town. This is laying the ground for more expansion. So again they are putting infrastructure in place. When the time will come, all the infrastructure will be there and the oil companies will be ready to go. I pay attention to these issues."

"What will you do in the future if this development happens?" Sandeep asked, setting down a fork fully loaded with tasty moose.

"It may not happen during my lifetime. You have to fight in the right way," Robert replied. However, Robert did tell us that First Nations in the region were reaching out to the international community to protect their rights. In December 2014, the Mikisew Cree First Nation petitioned UNESCO to place Wood Buffalo National Park on the List of World Heritage in Danger, due to the impacts of hydroelectric dams on the Peace River, including the new Site C dam, harm from oil sands development and potential harm from a new proposed oil sands mine, threats from climate change, and a lack of sufficient monitoring.[98]

UNESCO took the petition seriously and agreed to send a reactive monitoring mission of experts in September 2016 to assess threats to the park. In March 2017, UNESCO issued a warning to Canada, saying that it would add the park to the List of World Heritage in Danger unless area management improved. Its report states, "There is long-standing, conceivable and consistent evidence of severe environmental and human health concerns based on both western science and local and indigenous knowledge," and "the concerns coincide with the absence of effective and independent mechanisms to analyze and address these concerns at an adequate scale."[99]

We told Robert about some of the conversations we had in Fort Chipewyan about a transition away from fossil fuels to renewables. When we asked Robert if he would be interested in working in the renewable energy sector, he said, "I would love to have a job in the renewable energy industry. But where's the job?"

After our time with Robert in Fort McMurray, we reflected on the past months. Our visit to the coal mining areas in India and the oil sands in Canada made it clear to us that, just as it was important to speak to people in areas dependent on fossil fuel, if we didn't speak to people who were working hard to bring about an increasingly renewable world, we'd only have half the picture. We decided to spend the second year of our master's program exploring the global transition to renewable energy, and its future. We wanted to understand how real the transition to renewable energy is, and what a new renewable world might look like. We also wanted to understand whether this transition would take the current fossil fuel workforce into account by accommodating them either in new renewable industries or in other occupations. We spent the following months exploring these questions by talking to people at the forefront of the renewable energy transition.

*Part IV*

———

# JOURNEY FORWARD

## Chapter Eight

# THE RENEWABLE REVOLUTION

*We keep being told that the answer to our problems is an amazing new technology, and we keep looking somewhere else for the answer, when it's in our hands the whole time. Talk about getting your power back! ... This is power to the people – literally and metaphorically.*

—Andrew Moore, solar project director
at T'Sou-ke First Nation

"After the Paris conference, everyone knows why we have to do something about the climate, and some know what to do, but very few people know exactly how to do it. So that's what's holding everyone up. You just need to get out and do it," said Andrew Moore, solar project director at T'Sou-ke First Nation. We'd driven out to T'Sou-ke First Nation to meet Andrew, a tall man with a relaxed demeanour, white curly hair and an English accent. He pointed to a huge solar array in front of us, soaking up the strong August sun. "What we're trying to do is show that there is another way to do it – and it's the Aboriginal way," he told us. "If you go back to the values of First Nations and take them forward – if you go back to this basic respect-ful appreciation of each other and everyone else who lives on the Earth, once you do that, then you've got a real chance of finding a sustainable path forward. So that's really what we are trying to do – First Nations leading the way to being sustain-able once more."

T'Sou-ke First Nation, located on the southern tip of Vancouver Island in British Columbia, Canada, has a registered population of about 250 people living on two reserves (67 hectares total) that were allotted by the government in 1877. The elected chief, Gordon Planes, has helped lead the way for the nation's innovative solar projects and other sustainable initiatives, such as a successful wasabi greenhouse project, where wasabi is grown for commercial sale.

Although T'Sou-ke only began its journey towards renewable energy in 2008, it has already produced so much power from solar energy that it's selling it back to the electricity grid during the summer. Andrew – who is not from T'Sou-ke First Nation but has worked for them for years – helped lead a community-visioning exercise in 2008 that engaged everyone in the community, even children, to come together and chart out the nation's path for the future.

The planning was based on the seventh-generation principle – planning 100 years into the future. The visioning identified four priorities: food security, cultural renaissance, economic self-sufficiency and energy security. Once the mandate from the community was clear, Andrew told us that everything happened sort of serendipitously, with determination and a little bit of luck. The British Columbia Ministry of Energy and Mines created an Innovative Clean Energy Fund, and T'Sou-ke turned in a winning proposal in the first funding round. This funding only partially met its needs for its first solar project. However, the financial support of the ministry helped the project truly get going, and T'Sou-ke found the rest of the funding along the way.

For the solar project, T'Sou-ke installed a total of 440 photovoltaic solar panels that provide 75 kilowatts of power. The nation installed a 6-kilowatt system on the roof of the fisheries office, a 7-kilowatt system on the roof of the band hall, and the largest, a 62-kilowatt system, on top of and beside the canoe shed. When the project was rolled out, it was the largest community solar project in British Columbia. Since then, T'Sou-ke has also put a solar hot-water heating program in place for residences, put systems on the roofs of 40 houses, installed a solar-powered electric charging point for vehicles in front of the administration office and carried out a comprehensive energy conservation program.

What is so remarkable about T'Sou-ke's solar project is that the nation has accomplished much more with it than just achieving "net zero" for the administration buildings and a few houses (meaning they produce as much power as they consume) and reducing hot water electricity bills for residences. It has also managed to generate lasting employment for community members. When T'Sou-ke searched for a contractor to carry out the solar project, it wanted someone who would be willing to train and employ community members for the project. As a result, 12 community members were trained as solar installers by a Victoria-based contractor, Home Energy Solutions.

As we stood in front of the solar array, chatting, Andrew laughed. "The contractor from Home Energy Solutions told us it's most unusual that we employ our own client! But it worked quite well." Our ears perked up at the word *employment*. "Each month, when we were doing the installation, Home Energy Solutions would send us a bill for work done in that month, and then we'd send them a bill for employing our guys and girls," he told us. As the community progressed to the solar hot-water heating project and the energy conservation project, the same community members remained involved, and others joined in the work too. The experience working on the community solar project has given some members the opportunity to find employment outside the community. Following the solar panel installation, the community members trained at T'Sou-ke First Nation received a special Canadian Solar Industries Association (CanSIA) training and worked on a large 1,000-house project in neighbouring Colwood.

What's more, T'Sou-ke is making money from its solar panels. Because the community first built the solar panel system and later carried out the energy conservation measures, the panels actually generate more electricity than the administration buildings need. Andrew told us that, given the chance, they'd do it the other way around next time – taking the energy efficiency measures first.

T'Sou-ke is connected to the electricity grid, which allows it to sell electricity to BC Hydro (a government-owned company that supplies the province with electricity) and buy it back when they need it. "On a day like today, we're probably selling from eight in the morning to eight at night. Although in the middle of winter, we buy some of it back," Andrew said. He pointed up to the sun. "There's a phrase Chief Gordon uses: when we have a solar spill in our community, we call it a very nice day!"

T'Sou-ke isn't finished yet. It has many irons in the fire and is keen to get its energy efficiency and renewable energy model out in the world and scaled up. It is working with the University of Victoria (UVic) on the business case for this type of community solar power model. UVic, Savannah's alma mater, is about an hour's drive from the reserve. T'Sou-ke is also actively pursuing other forms of renewable energy. It has partnered with Accumulated Ocean Energy Inc. to explore the possibilities of ocean wave energy production and is also exploring the possibility of a kite energy demonstration project.

As we left the solar array, and Andrew locked the chain link fence behind us, he said, "We keep being told that the answer to our problems is an amazing new technology, and we keep looking somewhere else for the answer, when it's in our hands the whole time. Talk about getting your power back!" He shook his head. "This is power to the people – literally and metaphorically."

◆

It was 7:30 a.m., and we'd managed to drag ourselves out of bed and get outside. It was absolutely freezing. "It's nice to be out!" said Savannah. She comes from a family of outdoorsy people, and everyone in her family loves to be out in nature.

"It was nice inside. Some nice, warm breakfast would have been a great start to the day," Sandeep said as we began our run. Sandeep's family loves their food.

Since we first met, we'd realized that we come from completely different cultures. During our time in India and Canada, we managed to introduce each other to our families. In India, staying with Sandeep's family for three weeks, we gained five kilograms each, thanks to the wonderful Indian food. Anyone who has been to or lived in India can understand this. In Canada, we lost all the kilograms we gained – all the nature hikes, biking, running and fresh, vegetable-laden meals did it.

We were in Lund, a student town in the south of Sweden, where we were completing the third semester of our master's program. Only a few days had passed since we'd visited the T'Sou-ke First Nation in Canada. It was early September. As we began our run, we passed a few international student housing complexes. After about ten minutes, we reached some fields on the outskirts of town. The stories from T'Sou-ke were fresh in our minds, and we were more curious about renewable energy than ever before. The fields were green, and the groves of trees surrounding them were spectacularly beautiful. Turning a corner, we saw a series of wind towers in the distance. As we ran further, their numbers increased and we realized how massive they are – something that's difficult to gauge from a photograph.

That was day one. For the next four months in Sweden, we saw hundreds of those wind towers. We also visited Copenhagen, the capital of Denmark, a 45-minute train ride from Lund. And these wind towers wouldn't leave us – it was as if they followed us everywhere. During the train ride from Lund to Copenhagen, across the Øresund Bridge, the Baltic Sea was marked by offshore wind towers, their blades slowly spinning and producing clean, green energy.

During our time in Scandinavia, we wondered whether this renewable energy transition was limited to rich countries. We saw that small, wealthy countries like Sweden are able to provide reliable electricity for their citizens using renewables. For them, replacing one electricity source with another – replacing fossil fuels with renewables – is comparatively easy. Yet we knew large numbers of people in countries like India still lived without any power at all. How difficult would it be for them to transition to renewables? Can countries reduce or eliminate their reliance on fossil fuels and make a transition to renewable energy, while also finding ways to provide electricity to people living off-grid?

We decided to try to explore this topic during our final semester after Sweden, which was set aside for master's thesis research. We knew we wanted to focus on one of the most promising technological developments helping light rural areas in poor countries without access to the electricity grid – solar lighting products. There were two big roadblocks. First, we wanted to conduct research and write our thesis together, so that we could tackle a larger-than-usual question: our plan was to investigate the diffusion of off-grid solar lighting products in a comparative study of two countries with very different market development. Yet, as far as we knew, no one in our department had ever done a joint thesis, and we weren't even sure if it was possible. Second, we needed funding to carry out field research, because we wanted to conduct interviews in both countries with key stakeholders. Otherwise we'd have to resign ourselves to writing a well-researched thought experiment from a desk in Sweden. Undaunted, we decided to approach Professor Aleh Cherp, our program coordinator and a professor whose research centres on energy transitions, with our idea.

Early on during our time in Sweden, we let Aleh know that we'd like to meet with him to discuss an out-of-the box thesis proposal. Meeting over lunch one sunny day in Lund, we pitched our thesis idea to him. We told him that we wanted to understand how the transition to renewables such as solar was happening in poor, rural areas where people still depended on kerosene, a petroleum product. To do it, we wanted to visit

Kenya and the northern state of Bihar, India, places where more than 80 per cent of the rural population lives without electricity, and where markets for off-grid solar lighting products have developed very differently. We also wanted to travel to San Francisco, where a large cluster of companies working in both India and Kenya had offices, to get a comparative perspective on the markets. To our surprise and delight, Aleh fully supported our idea. He told us that our approach was how many researchers worked nowadays – for example, collaborating on academic journal articles. However, we'd have to produce two separate theses with distinct content. We agreed, and he also offered to help us find funding.

A few weeks after that meeting, it still wasn't clear whether we'd find funding. As we continued to refine our thesis idea, reality started to intrude – we'd need to book plane tickets soon, and Sandeep needed to start applying for the difficult and time-consuming US visa, or we wouldn't be able to do our field research regardless of whether we received the full amount of funding we'd requested. Taking a leap of faith, we booked our tickets to India for the first part of our research, and Sandeep started working on the visa.

A few weeks later, on a cold November day, Aleh invited us to a meeting at the International Institute of Industrial Environmental Economics, the institute where we took our courses at Lund University. It was past four p.m., which in Sweden meant it was pitch black and chilly. Sitting around a table while the wind whistled outside the windows, Aleh told us he'd secured funding for us that would cover our research costs. He cautioned us that with the funding came responsibility – and that we should really dedicate ourselves to the research over the coming months to make it a success.

With that green light, we threw our all into our thesis research and gathered some fascinating insights in our final semester. We started our interviews in Bihar in January, travelled to Kenya in February, and then finished off the interviews in March in the United States. We discovered that in both Bihar and Kenya, people who until recently had never seen electricity in their lives are now using off-grid solar lighting products such as solar home systems. Some install small solar systems on their roofs, providing enough power for basic lighting and running small entertainment devices like radios. Another popular product is the smaller, cheaper solar lantern, which charges in the sun and provides light at night.

This is really positive, because solar lighting products are replacing traditional lighting products like kerosene lamps, which, in addition to running on fossil fuel and contributing to global warming, also harm people's health and cause hazards like fires. The transition from kerosene lamps to solar lighting products also has the potential to create a lot of jobs – over and above the number of jobs eliminated, as kerosene takes a back seat to solar. In a 2016 study, researcher Evan Mills at the University of California's Lawrence Berkeley National Laboratory found that off-grid solar lighting products have the potential to create an estimated two million jobs across the developing world, taking into account jobs lost that are associated with traditional lighting sources such as kerosene.[100]

Many companies from around the world are now selling these solar products, even in very rural and isolated areas of poorer countries. Of the two places we researched, we found that Kenya is the undisputed leader. About 30 per cent of people in Kenya now use some kind of solar product in their households. Poor people there are able to afford solar products because companies are selling them using an innovative pay-as-you-go business model. Pay-as-you-go (PAYG) has recently taken the Kenyan off-grid solar market by storm. Customers make small payments for their installed solar system over a period of months or years until they eventually own the system. Products that were previously the preserve of the rural rich suddenly are available to many. What we witnessed in Kenya opened our eyes to a different shade of the renewable energy transition: some people were skipping grid electricity as a source of energy and moving directly to distributed renewables.

In February 2017, we were in the Nairobi office of Mobisol, a German off-grid solar products company that supplies solar home systems in several East African countries. Every 30 seconds the phone rang. "Hello, Mobisol Solar. How can I help you?" the phone attendant asked each time. The calls were from customers across Kenya, inquiring about different solar home systems. Once the customer told the attendant what they wanted, the attendant interviewed the customer for about ten minutes to evaluate their financial capacity and credit history. If the customer qualified, the attendant offered them a certain size of solar home system along with a payment package. "Our people are trained to ask the right questions in order to create a customer profile. After evaluation of the customer's financial background, each customer is offered a PAYG package for a solar home system," explained Cedrick Todwell, the marketing manager at Mobisol Kenya.

Cedrick added that affordability was a big issue before 2011. Only rich people could afford solar home systems or solar lanterns. But then, in 2011, things started to change. Cedrick explained that by riding on the success of mobile money and the development of machine-to-machine connectivity technology, PAYG business models have revolutionized the off-grid solar sector in Kenya. He elaborated: "Paying US$200 or US$300 upfront for a solar home system is very difficult for most rural customers. But if they are told they can pay 50 cents a day, most people are able to afford it." Most PAYG companies in Kenya try to match the payment the customer makes for the solar product with what they would have paid anyway for kerosene, or offer an even more favourable rate. We spoke to the leader of one non-profit initiative in western Kenya providing solar lanterns, who described her model. In Kenya, kerosene is not subsidized, and an average off-grid household spends about 50 Kenyan shillings (KSH) (approx. US$0.48) a day on it. In contrast, the PAYG solar lanterns that the non-profit initiative provides to villagers cost about 30 KSH (approx. US$0.29) per day. And, as an added bonus, this lantern payment plan is pay-to-own – so after about five to six months, the consumer has paid off the lantern and owns it. One company we interviewed told us that expensive, unsubsidized kerosene "makes our proposal compelling."

We were fascinated to learn that one of the biggest differences between the lagging Bihar market in India and the surging Kenyan market was a successful business model, based on mobile money and machine-to-machine connectivity technology.

In 2007, major Kenyan telecom company Safaricom launched mobile money in Kenya and named it M-Pesa. Karen Basiye, senior manager of sustainability and social policy at Safaricom (and former graduate of MESPOM, our master's program) told us how mobile money works. "Mobile money" (now synonymous with "M-Pesa") refers to mobile-phone-operated virtual banking networks that allow customers with mobile money accounts to make payments or transfer money using their cell phones. This allows "unbanked" people from both rural and urban areas to access a type of banking facility that may have been previously unavailable. "It doesn't matter whether they have bank accounts or not, you just top up money in your M-Pesa account and use that money to buy products or transfer money to others," said Karen.

While mobile money was the trigger, off-grid solar companies in Kenya were also innovative. They either developed their own machine-to-machine connectivity technology or bought it from technology providers. In Nairobi, we interviewed another MESPOM alumna, Purnima Kumar, who works for Lumeter, a company providing PAYG technology solutions for companies. She told us that Lumeter provides companies with the two necessary aspects of a PAYG system: one, a chip for manufacturers that they put in a product to enable PAYG; and two, a software platform that distributors can use to manage a PAYG business. Companies install the chips (the same radio technology used in cell phones) in solar devices like solar home systems, and use the combination of chip and software to remotely control the system, monitor its function, process payments and turn off the system when customer credit runs out. The combination of mobile money payments and machine-to-machine connectivity technology allows companies with PAYG business models to easily deliver solar power to rural customers.

We interviewed Nikhil Nair, the director of sales at leading Kenyan off-grid solar home system company M-Kopa. He explained that, in Kenya, if a customer has an issue with an M-Kopa system, they can call the company line, and the machine-to-machine technology system will help the company determine the cause of the problem – for example, they can see if the battery isn't working, or if the issue is that the solar panel is in the shade. "It's phenomenal," he told us. "And, there's nothing like that in India."

He described how a leading Indian solar home system company struggled without the benefit of machine-to-machine technology. "There, every time someone called to say something's not working, the company had to get a guy [to] go to the customer's house on a bus to figure out what was wrong and return the next day." We were astounded by this information. It was clear to us that solar technology, along with an innovative business model, was disrupting the kerosene economy in Kenya. Tony Seba, an energy expert and professor at Stanford University, wrote in his book, *Clean Disruption of Energy and Transportation*, "Most people think of market disruption in terms of 'disruptive technologies.' Many times, however, the source of disruption is not a new technology per se but an innovative business model made possible using a new technology."[101]

We learned that it is not just individuals who are seeing the benefits of solar power. Many communities in countries like Kenya and India are coming together to install solar mini-grids. In January 2016, Chhotkei village, located in the eastern state of Odisha, became India's first smart village powered by Nanogrid technology. Before this initiative, the villagers of Chhotkei lived without electricity. SunMoksha, an Indian company, supplied the village with a 30-kilowatt solar-powered smart Nanogrid to meet its electricity demands. Now 140 houses, 20 streetlights, a temple and three community centres glow brightly at night. A part of the generated electricity is also used for irrigation and used by micro-enterprises operating in the village.

It almost seemed like a silent energy transition had begun! But was it really silent? More and more, global attention is being drawn to this issue. In December 2015, at the UN Climate Change Conference in Paris, 195 countries collectively decided to limit global warming to well below two degrees Celsius. The Renewable Energy Policy Network *Global Status Report* for 2016 claims, "Out of the 189 countries that submitted Intended Nationally Determined Contributions (INDCs), 147 countries mentioned renewable energy, and 167 countries mentioned energy efficiency; in addition, some countries committed to reforming their subsidies for fossil fuels. Precedent-setting commitments to renewable energy also were made by regional, state and local governments as well as by the private sector."[102] Top energy-consuming countries made commitments to increase the share of renewables in their energy mix. It's clear that communities and individuals at one level, and countries on another, are showcasing their commitment to renewable energy. The shift is happening.

China, the world's largest greenhouse gas emitter, committed to increase the share of non-fossil fuels in its energy consumption to 20 per cent by 2030 as part of the Paris talks. The country also made a commitment during the Paris conference that, by 2030, it would lower its $CO_2$ emissions per unit of GDP to 60 per cent – 65 per cent of 2005 levels. In our day-to-day world, these commitments mean a huge boost for renewable energy in China – more solar, more wind. Some experts are hailing China as an upcoming renewable energy superpower.

The world's second-largest greenhouse gas emitter, the United States, also made similar commitments. According to the nationally determined contribution (NDC) submitted by the United States after the Paris conference, "The United States intends to achieve an economy-wide target of reducing its greenhouse gas emissions by 26-28 per cent below its 2005 level in 2025 and to make best efforts to reduce its emissions by 28%."[103]

However, in March 2017, newly elected United States President Donald Trump, who has claimed climate change is a hoax perpetrated by the Chinese, signed an executive order rolling back former President Obama's Clean Power Plan, an essential environmental action agenda that was crucial to the United States' ability to meet its Paris pledge.

In March, during our thesis semester, we spent time in California, at the Middlebury Institute of International Studies at Monterey. While there, we met several research scholars who told us that even Trump's election and his endorsements of the fossil fuel industry were not likely to stop the ongoing shift to renewables. Against a dark backdrop of Trump's pro-fossil-fuel policies, hopeful developments still abounded. In May 2017, Atlanta became the 27th city in the United States to commit to obtaining 100 per cent of its electricity from renewable sources like wind and solar power, part of a growing movement.

Then, in June 2017, President Trump announced that the United States would withdraw from the Paris Agreement, stating that he wanted to renegotiate a deal he claimed would disadvantage United States' businesses and workers. He famously stated, "I was elected to represent the citizens of Pittsburgh, not Paris."

Trump's decision was followed by a swift outcry across the world as other countries, as well as United States cities, states and businesses, decried the decision and reaffirmed their commitment to fight climate change. Many promised to step up and take even more action than before. France, Germany and Italy quickly put out a joint statement that said the Paris agreement was not renegotiable. German Chancellor Angela Merkel called Trump's decision "extremely regrettable" and reaffirmed Germany's commitment to the Paris Agreement and to tackling climate change.[104] Her remarks were matched by similar statements from other countries, including Canada and France.

In addition, a coalition of nine states, 125 cities, 183 colleges and universities and 902 businesses and investors released a statement announcing their formation of a coalition called "We Are Still In" and stating that they would work together to step up to fight climate change, since the federal government would not. In addition, 12 states and Puerto Rico committed to upholding the Paris Agreement by forming the United States Climate Alliance, while 211 Climate Mayors (a coalition of United States mayors taking action on climate change) committed to upholding the Paris Agreement goals (the number of mayors has since grown to over 380). Even the mayor of Pittsburgh fired back a rebuttal at Trump, saying the city would continue to follow Paris Agreement guidelines. It remains to be seen how President Trump's actions will affect the United States' ability to meet its Paris commitments.[105]

The European Union (EU) is the world's third-largest emitter. Its Paris NDC committed the EU and its member states to a binding target of an at least 40 per cent domestic reduction in greenhouse gas emissions by 2030 compared to 1990. However, it's no surprise that the EU has been a climate leader for a while. In 2009, the EU passed the Renewable Energy Directive, requiring EU countries to obtain at least 20 per cent of their final energy consumption from renewables by 2020.

India, the fourth-largest emitter, made a pledge to produce 40 per cent of its electricity from non-fossil-fuel-based energy resources by 2030. The country has also committed to reducing its emissions intensity by 33 to 35 per cent measured against a baseline of 2005.

Canada also makes the list of top ten emitters. Incredible, right? Despite the country's relatively small population of 36 million (for comparison, India's population is 1.3 billion), Canada is a big emitter. In its Paris pledge, Canada committed to "achieve an economy-wide target to reduce its greenhouse gas emissions by 30% below 2005 levels by 2030."[106]

These numbers may not mean much to an average person, but they represent an unprecedented historical shift in the way the world intends to generate and consume energy. These changes are timely, and desperately needed. However, even if they are adhered to, they may not be enough.

In 2016, the United Nations Environment Programme released a report stating that even if every country that pledged to cut emissions in Paris keeps its promise (which is unlikely), the world will still fall short of its target of keeping warming below two degrees Celsius. At best, the individual commitments that have been made would only keep warming below three degrees Celsius.[107] However, built into the international climate talk process is a chance for countries to increase their ambitions and strengthen their targets over the coming years.[108] Despite worldwide interest in renewables, avoiding dangerous global warming will depend a great deal on political commitment, ambition, scientific progress, public support and technological development over the coming years.

Some inspiring stories of strong commitment are already out there. Countries like Costa Rica and Iceland have already transitioned to nearly 100 per cent renewable electricity. Another country that is marching towards renewable energy is Denmark. This Scandinavian nation is blessed with unusually high winds and has at times produced almost 140 per cent of its electricity needs using wind power – with excess power being exported to Germany, Norway and Sweden. When we read about Denmark and renewable energy, we couldn't stop thinking about the wind towers that chased us during our time in Scandinavia.

Overall, the good news is that renewables are growing fast. In 2016, the International Energy Agency (IEA) upgraded its five-year growth forecast for renewables, citing strong policy support in key countries such as the US, China, India and Mexico, and sharp cost reductions in renewables. The IEA stated, "About half a million solar panels were installed *every day* around the world last year. In China, which accounted for about half the wind additions and 40% of all renewable capacity increases, two wind turbines were installed *every hour* in 2015."[109]

Two of the renewable sources advancing the fastest are wind and solar. The installed price of solar energy has already dropped significantly and is predicted to drop further in coming years.[110] In September 2016, the world was taken by surprise when a Chinese solar panel maker and a Japanese developer put in a bid to build the 350-megawatt Sweihan solar farm near Abu Dhabi for 2.42 US cents per kilowatt hour. This was remarkable because not only was it the lowest solar farm bid made yet, it also put the price of solar energy below that of gas or coal, which was about seven US cents per kilowatt hour at the time.[111] Suddenly, solar energy could compete with fossil fuels.

Prices for wind have also declined. In February 2015, a Swedish company, Vattenfall AB, won a contract from the Danish government to build the world's cheapest offshore wind farm in the North Sea, slated for completion in 2018. More of those wind towers! "Maybe Scandinavia's going to become a tourist destination for wind tower watchers," Savannah joked when we read about this.

You might have heard about solar panels and wind farms – but did you know that researchers are continually pushing the frontiers of what these technologies can do, and how they can be integrated into our everyday lives and landscapes? During our semester in Sweden, we had a class where we, along with our brilliant classmates, were invited to make a presentation showcasing one of these new technologies. One innovative idea that really caught our attention was the idea of solar roads – using highways to produce solar energy. This idea is still experimental, but it's catching on. In the United States, the State of Missouri agreed to let an Idaho start-up company, Solar Roadways, install special solar panels in the sidewalk close to the state's Route 66 rest stop. These solar panels are designed to be driven and walked over. They will generate energy, but also heat up as cars drive over them – eliminating the need for snow clearing in winter. Further, they have the potential to light up and communicate with drivers, replacing the need for street signs. Other solar road tests are occurring around the world, including in the Netherlands and France.[112]

Innovative ideas are also emerging in the field of wind energy. Several companies have come forward with the idea of kite power – generating electricity using giant kites in the sky. We'd first heard about this idea when we visited T'Sou-ke First Nation. One such company, the United Kingdom–based Kite Power Solutions, has developed a wind kite technology that it says could supply renewable energy at such low prices it would essentially halve the cost of offshore wind energy and not require any taxpayer subsidies. It also states that the kites can be deployed further offshore than conventional wind turbines, opening up new spaces to generate renewable energy, and can fly to greater heights than wind turbines can achieve, reaching stronger and more consistent winds.[113]

Kite Power Solutions' model generates electricity using two giant kites (up to 70 square metres each), which are attached to a turbine and released one at a time. As one kite is released, it rises up to 450 metres, moving in a figure-eight shape and pulling out a cable that turns the turbine, generating electricity. As the first kite goes up, the other comes down, meaning that the kites work in tandem and the system almost constantly generates electricity. This technology is already being piloted – Kite Power Solutions planned to open the first "kite power plant" in Scotland in 2017.[114] This means that a region of Scotland will soon be partly powered by kites. While this will only be a 500-kilowatt demonstration system, the company has plans to build a larger, three-megawatt system after that, and to generate several hundred megawatts by 2025.[115]

"If all these technological advancements work out, in the future when we go for a run we might be doing it on solar roads with wind kites in the distance!" Sandeep said. "And of course there will be fields of wind towers alongside," he laughed as we finished our run that evening.

Sandeep and Savannah inside the Argada underground coal mine in central Jharkhand. As we walked down into the mine, we used hand-held flashlights roped to our bodies to light the way, and a pointed stick to keep our balance. PHOTO: PARWAZ AHMED KHAN

With Giriraj Kumar, the young overman of the Argada underground coal mine (to the right of Sandeep), Arun Kumar Singh, the trade union leader (behind Savannah), and two other coal mine workers. Every day, mine workers must walk down slippery, unlit steps to the depths of the mine to extract coal. PHOTO: PARWAZ AHMED KHAN

In Jharkhand, parents who work in coal mines often bring their children to help them. Here, workers are shown loading coal into trucks to be transported off-site. PHOTO: PARWAZ AHMED KHAN

Coal-cycle *wallahs* carry up to 450 kilograms of coal per bicycle, and may push their bicycles 60 kilometres over hilly terrain to reach their destination. PHOTO: PARWAZ AHMED KHAN

After scavenging for coal, the coal-cycle *wallahs* and their families wash the coal to eliminate ash and other debris, then cook it in burning, smoking piles near their homes. This softens the coal and increases its quality, so it can be sold for a higher price. On average, the coal-cycle *wallah* and their family make a living of US$10 per week. PHOTO: PARWAZ AHMED KHAN

Massive coal fires burn close to Kumhar *basti*, sending huge plumes of white smoke and gas up into the air. Residents of Kumhar *basti* live their lives amidst the smoke and poisonous gases. PHOTO: PARWAZ AHMED KHAN

A view of open-cast coal mining in Jharia, amidst smoke from coal fires in the mine. PHOTO: PARWAZ AHMED KHAN

Suresh Bhuiyan, a Jharia coal worker, and his wife Srikumari Devi, along with two of their daughters and several of their grandchildren. The picture was taken at Suresh and Srikumari's eldest daughter's house. They moved in after their house was flooded with water from a nearby pond.

PHOTO: PARWAZ AHMED KHAN

Mining overburden burns in Dhanbad, the administrative capital of the Jharia region, producing smoke combined with steam from recent rain. PHOTO: PARWAZ AHMED KHAN

Suresh Bhuiyan shows us his flooded house (on the left). He is no longer able to live there. PHOTO: PARWAZ AHMED KHAN

Savannah touching the ground in Golakd *basti*, Jharia.
The ground was hot because of the underground coal fires below.
PHOTO: PARWAZ AHMED KHAN

The pond at the centre of Golakd *basti*. The woman and child pictured are washing dishes in the pond's polluted water. Women also wash clothes in the pond. PHOTO: PARWAZ AHMED KHAN

Srikumari Devi used to scavenge coal but had to stop because of her poor health. Now she raises pigs, ducks and chickens. During the day, she works hard to protect them from dogs and vultures.
PHOTO: PARWAZ AHMED KHAN

When we met Titri Devi, a resident of Golakd *basti*, she was pregnant. She told us that it is hard to bear the heat from the underground fires, and the coal dust blowing into the settlement from the nearby mines.
PHOTO: PARWAZ AHMED KHAN

Dananjee Sharma, Golakd *basti*'s young barber, shows us where he was trapped in the floor of his bedroom after the land subsided and the walls and floor of his house cracked. He was trapped there for ten minutes, crying out for help, before someone came to rescue him.
PHOTO: PARWAZ AHMED KHAN

A house in Jharia with a large poster of the Hindu goddess Durga. Many residents of Jharia put up posters like this because they hope the gods will prevent the land from subsiding beneath their house. PHOTO: PARWAZ AHMED KHAN

Speaking with Santosh Bhuiyan (sitting to the right of Sandeep) in Golakd *basti*. PHOTO: PARWAZ AHMED KHAN

Young boys near Golakd *basti* scavenge large chunks of coal. They will carry the coal home, where their parents will cook the coal to prepare it for sale. PHOTO: PARWAZ AHMED KHAN

Santosh points out the metre-wide coal fire crater near Golakd *basti*.
PHOTO: PARWAZ AHMED KHAN

A view of Belgoria, the new township where the government is resettling people from Jharia. PHOTO: PARWAZ AHMED KHAN

People walk through an open-cast mine in Jharia, close to visible coal fires in the mine. PHOTO: PARWAZ AHMED KHAN

A few months before we arrived in Fort McMurray, the north-eastern Alberta town that is the beating heart of Canadian oil sands extraction, a massive wildfire broke out nearby and the town was evacuated. The picture shows one of the neighbour-hoods destroyed in the fire.

A tailings pond in the midst of the oil sands. Tailings ponds are artificial bodies of water that store the waste water left over when bitumen is extracted from the oil sands. According to the Pembina Institute, a leading Canadian environmental think tank, tailings ponds currently cover more than 220 square kilometres of northern Alberta, amounting to one trillion litres of fluid tailings.

An aerial shot of part of an oil sands mine near Fort McMurray, Alberta.

An oil sands operation near Fort McMurray, Alberta. Natural Resources Canada reports that the oil sands account for 9.3 per cent of Canada's greenhouse gas emissions, which means they produce more greenhouse gas emissions than many small countries, such as Sweden.

An oil sands operation at a distance, near Fort McMurray, Alberta.

Part of an oil sands operation near Fort McMurray, Alberta. Alberta's oil reserves are an estimated 166 billion barrels – the third-largest oil reserves in the world, after Saudi Arabia and Venezuela.

Robert Grandjambe, a fourth generation trapper, hunter and member of the Mikisew Cree First Nation.
PHOTO: ROBERT GRANDJAMBE

Robert Grandjambe cooking his meal after hunting.
PHOTO: ROBERT GRANDJAMBE

Robert Grandjambe prepares to skin a lynx he caught.
PHOTO: ROBERT GRANDJAMBE

Robert Grandjambe was 6 years old when he started helping his father set their trapline. In this photo, a young Robert displays some of his furs.
PHOTO: ROBERT GRANDJAMBE

An aerial view of Fort Chipewyan, a community more than 200 kilometres north of Fort McMurray, and downstream from the oil sands.

Part of the Peace-Athabasca Delta (PAD), one of the world's largest inland deltas. The PAD forms at the confluence of the Peace, Athabasca and Birch rivers, west of Lake Athabasca in northern Alberta. The delta is considered by many to be the heart of northern Alberta's vast Wood Buffalo National Park.

T'Sou-ke First Nation has installed a solar-powered electric charging point for vehicles in front of the administration office, and owns an electric car that community members can use.

A shopkeeper in Ranchi, India, shows Sandeep a solar lantern. Many people in countries like India and Kenya, who until recently had never seen electricity in their lives, are now using off-grid solar lighting products such as solar lanterns. These products are replacing traditional kerosene lamps.

T'Sou-ke First Nation, located on the southern tip of Vancouver Island in British Columbia, Canada, is transitioning to renewable energy. They produce so much power from solar energy that they are selling it back to the electricity grid during the summer.

Wind turbines at a distance in Lund, Sweden, the location of the third semester of our master's program.

Sandeep and Savannah in front of the new Central European
University building in Budapest, during their last few days
in the city at the end of their master's program.

# Chapter Nine

# LAST HURDLES

*Sunlight is everywhere. A combination of wind, solar, hydro etc. can generate electricity for the world. In the long run, we can be fossil-fuel-free in the electricity sector. However, transportation fuel is still a big challenge.*
    —Vaclav Smil, scientist and energy transitions expert

"So what's the angle of your book?" he asked us over the phone. We were thrilled to be doing this interview. We'd first been introduced to his influential work during our master's course, and since had read many of his articles and books.

"We want to explore the stories of people who live and work in fossil-fuel-rich areas, their economic dependency on fossil fuel extraction, the environmental and health impacts of living in those areas, and what a transition to renewable energy will look like for them," Sandeep replied.

To us he was the guru of energy transitions studies. Talking to him for our book was like talking to the Barack Obama of the energy world. He was Vaclav Smil, a scientist and energy transitions expert, whom Microsoft founder Bill Gates described as the "author whose books he most looks forward to." We had a lot of questions for him. Did solar, wind and other renewable sources have the potential to replace fossil fuels? What challenges did the renewable energy transition face, and how could it overcome them? And what about the employment question – how could the world smoothly transition to renewables?

We asked him if he thinks it's possible to have a total transition to renewable energy. Vaclav replied, "Sunlight is everywhere. A combination of wind, solar, hydro etc. can generate electricity for the world. In the long run, we can be fossil-fuel-free in the electricity sector. However, transportation fuel is still a big challenge."

Vaclav elaborates on this point in his book, *Energy Transitions: Global and National Perspectives.*[116] He writes that the potential energy from solar radiation absorbed by land is roughly 2,000 times the energy produced from current fossil fuel extraction. "Even after excluding polar and subpolar regions with the weakest insolation and the areas difficult to access (steep mountains, wetlands) there are still at least 15 PW of potentially usable flux, roughly 900 times today's annual fossil fuel consumption," he states in his book. Wind also has huge potential. Scientists from Stanford University and the University of Delaware estimate that from half to several times the world's all-purpose power can be generated using wind energy by the year 2030.[117]

Before going further, it's very important to understand a basic point about energy, which underlies a big unsolved problem. "People tend to confuse energy and electricity. While solar and wind sources can be used to produce electricity, which can power homes, air conditioners, washing machines and various other electrical devices, their use in the transportation sector is limited," Vaclav told us. This is a key issue because a great deal of the worldwide transportation sector (including cars, trucks, boats and planes) runs on petroleum products like gasoline, diesel fuel and jet fuel – not electricity. For example, in the United States in 2015, electricity provided less than 1 per cent of the total energy used in the transportation sector.[118] Depending on the method of transportation, the technology either doesn't exist, or exists only in nascent form, for replacing liquid fossil fuel with a renewable source of energy. Yet we can't ignore the transportation sector if we are serious about moving to a fossil-fuel-free world. The transportation sector today is responsible for about 14 per cent of global greenhouse gas emissions.[119]

There are a few possible ways of running transportation on something other than liquid fossil fuels. Two of the top candidates are electricity and biofuels. Some electricity technologies exist in the market – such as electric vehicles – and their presence is growing rapidly.

We were surprised to find out that electric vehicles are not a new technology. They have been around since the early 19th century, and by the end of the 19th century, almost 38 per cent of the cars in the United States ran on electricity. However, they disappeared from the roads when fossil-fuel-powered vehicles began to dominate the sector. Charles Morris, the author of a book on Tesla Motors, the California-based company seen as a pioneer in the electric vehicle business, writes, "The main drawback of EVs [electric vehicles] was the same as it is today – limited range, thanks to constraints of battery technology. As the network of roads expanded, this came to be seen as more of a problem." During the historical heyday of electric vehicles, gasoline-powered cars were considered smelly and loud, and starting them required a hand crank, which sometimes jammed and wrenched the user's arm. Charles writes that as the price of gasoline steadily became cheaper, and innovations like Hiram Percy Maxim's muffler (1897) and Charles Kettering's electric starter (1912) helped deal with existing issues with gasoline-powered vehicles, electric vehicles disappeared from the roads.[120]

However, electric vehicles have recently started to make a slow comeback. The International Energy Agency's 2016 *Global EV Outlook* report states that, in 2005, the number of electric cars was in the hundreds, but by 2015 more than one million electric cars were on the road. Overall, however, electric cars only represent 0.1 per cent of the global vehicle stock and are still struggling to overcome limitations, such as the range a car can travel before it needs to be recharged, and the cost of the car.[121]

One interesting development on the electric vehicle scene has been the emergence of Tesla Motors, which entered the car manufacturing market in 2003 with a focus on electric cars. Tesla has improved the range problem and added features to its electric vehicles that make them attractive to the public, such as free technology updates for the vehicle systems. "The performance of Tesla Model S equals that of the most venerated luxury sedans, and it happens to use no gasoline," Charles writes. He adds, "It has changed the way the public perceives electric vehicles and, perhaps most importantly, has inspired several much larger automotive industry players to redouble their electrification efforts."[122]

Some experts believe that even if electric vehicles become a viable option for personal consumer use in the future, the widespread use of electric vehicles in the trucking sector – which transports goods all over the world – will remain a challenge for a long time. "You have to segment the transportation sector. Where electric vehicles are going to be difficult is in heavy goods transport. It would be easier in two or four wheelers, or even in short duration public transport, because we could run city buses using electricity," said Chandra Bhushan, deputy director general of the Centre for Science and Environment, a leading think tank in India. He added, "Trucking will be difficult because of the range. If you want to eliminate trucking, then goods will need to be transported using railways. Trains already run on electricity, so this could be an option."

Beyond land-based vehicles, there have also been pilot demonstrations of solar planes and boats, but they are not yet near commercialization. In 2016, the Solar Impulse 2 – an aircraft – made history when it travelled 40,000 kilometres, circumnavigating the globe. Its only power source was the sun, charging more than 17,000 solar cells on its wings. The solar cells collected energy during the day, which was stored in large batteries that made up one quarter of the plane's weight. It travelled slowly, at only 140 kilometres per hour, compared to a Boeing 747's nearly 1000 kilometres per hour.[123]

Solar boats have also been making the news. In 2012, a solar boat called *PlanetSolar* successfully circumnavigated the globe, and, in 2016, a boat called *Energy Observer*, powered by a mix of solar, wind and hydrogen, set out to do the same. The success of something like a solar plane or solar boat (or eventually, solar ship) is significant – many people have to fly for work or want to fly for holidays, and we also depend on imported goods from other countries. "Swedes can import wind energy from Denmark; they could, let's say in the next 30 years, become a fossil-fuel-free electricity country," Vaclav said. "But can they produce steel without fossil fuel? Half of the teenagers in Sweden are flying to Thailand now. Can they use renewable energy to fly to Thailand?" He laughed. "Try to fly using wind turbines!"

Those are a few of the issues with electricity and transportation – but what about biofuels? There are several generations of biofuels, each with associated problems. "First generation" refers to biofuels derived from food-based crops, like ethanol from corn or sugarcane molasses, or biodiesel from soybean, rapeseed oil and palm oil. "Second generation" refers to those derived from non-food crops such as sugarcane crop residue, forest residues and jatropha. Both generations are plagued with issues: they are costly; they produce low net energy returns; they reduce carbon emissions less than expected; they raise food prices; they create an unsustainable demand for water and arable land. While they initially looked promising, they don't anymore.

The issues with first- and second-generation biofuels led to interest in a third generation of biofuels, this time based on algae as a feedstock. Researchers are generally positive about algae-based biofuel's potential, but the technology for cultivation and conversion is still in its infancy.[124] A fourth generation of biofuels is in the works, this time based on novel synthetic biology tools. It's expected that this generation could represent a fundamental breakthrough for biofuels, but it's still at the early research stage.[125]

Vaclav told us that, currently, "Modern societies still need liquid fuels. The only alternative to fossil fuel is biofuel." But the drawbacks are formidable. "In a country like India, where 200 million people are undernourished, and there are

50 million stunted children, the last thing you want to do is to plant biofuels."

The other major problem that Vaclav pointed out is the dependence of industry on fossil fuels. "It is difficult to make steel, ammonia and plastic without fossil fuels," he told us. "That's the biggest challenge."

For example, the steel industry requires a massive amount of fossil fuel. And this matters a lot because steel is a building block of modern societies – and we don't yet know how to produce it without fossil fuels. Steel is a key component of our railways, buildings, cars, appliances and heavy equipment such as bulldozers, and is also a component of cookware used in the home. The iron and steel industry is the largest industrial emitter of $CO_2$ in the world, responsible for 31 per cent of all industrial emissions.[126] Although advances in steel production have been made since the 1980s – for example, helping the steel industry reduce its energy use and water consumption – it still isn't clear how to produce steel without fossil fuels such as coal. For example, coal is used to produce coke, an important ingredient in steel production. Some interesting research has been done in Australia and New Zealand into producing a renewable, charcoal-based "green coke" to be used in steel production, but these initiatives are still in the trial phase.[127]

The story of cement is no different. The cement industry is responsible for 27 per cent of global industrial carbon emissions.[128] Cement, a fine powder, is produced from raw materials such as limestone, using a chemical process that releases large amounts of $CO_2$. Adding more emissions, cement is made in a cement kiln, which typically derives its heat from fossil fuels. Cement is a key ingredient in concrete, which is another vital building block of our modern world. When we interviewed Chandra, he told us, "It's a fundamental issue of materials. You cannot produce cement without releasing $CO_2$. It's a chemical reaction. Cement is a material that contributes to climate change."

What's also interesting and important about steel and

cement is that they are key components of many renewable energy technologies. Wind turbine towers are made from steel, they have a concrete base and, what's more, they have fibreglass blades – another fossil-fuel-dependent part. This is key. If we can't produce "green steel" using only renewable energy, develop $CO_2$-free alternatives to cement, or find a way to replace both completely, we can't produce some of the important nuts and bolts of renewable energy technology – and the world's transition will only ever be partway. Solving this dilemma will be a very important area for research and innovation in the future – for wind, and in many other areas. Even some types of mounts for solar panels use steel and concrete.

A final challenge few people think about is food. We can't produce food on the scale that we do nowadays without fossil fuel. One important reason is that fossil fuel is used to create nitrogen fertilizer. In his 2001 book, *Enriching the Earth: Fritz Haber, Carl Bosch, and the Transformation of World Food Production*, Vaclav estimates that, without nitrogen fertilizer, the world would be able to feed only 60 per cent of its population.[129] The key process that allows humans to create nitrogen fertilizer using fossil fuels is the Haber-Bosch process. Developed in the early 20th century, it allows humans to synthesize ammonia from the air using natural gas – a process that releases large amounts of $CO_2$. In turn, ammonia is used to produce other derivative products, such as urea, currently the most common type of nitrogen fertilizer.[130] As Chandra pointed out to us, "We don't know how to produce food without releasing $CO_2$. So far, all agriculture is dependent on fossil fuels in terms of urea. The entire fertilizer industry is dependent on urea. Agriculture is going to be a very difficult sector."

The good news is that some companies are working on developing fossil-fuel-free manufacturing of certain products. Tesla Motors opened its "Gigafactory" in 2016, which will produce enough batteries annually to power 500,000 electric cars. The factory will run entirely on renewable energy from solar, wind and geothermal. While this is just a preliminary step, and doesn't address all of the issues discussed above, it's the type of innovation the world needs to address the "fossil fuel ingredient" hurdle.

◆

After our conversation with Vaclav, we had a lot to think about. Fascinated by his description of the transportation and industry problem, we continued to think along these lines. "Those are important issues, sure," said Sandeep. "But there's more. What about wind and solar? The sun doesn't shine 24 hours a day, and the wind doesn't blow all the time."

We found that even with wind and solar, there are some significant challenges that will need to be overcome if we're going to depend on these technologies. Of the many issues, some of the most significant challenges include storage and grid stability.

First, storage. With fossil fuels, there is essentially no storage problem – we can burn fossil fuels 24 hours a day, 365 days a year to generate electricity. However, renewable energy like solar is different. It's intermittent, so you have to store the energy generated for later use. For example, the sun shines during the day, and when sunrays fall on photovoltaic panels, it generates electricity. However, if a village or a city is wholly dependent on solar energy for electricity, it won't have any electricity at night. One way to overcome this challenge is to store excess power, which can be used during periods when electricity is not actively being generated.

There are two main ways to store renewable energy (along with a third that's still in a nascent stage). The first method involves pumping water to a high elevation using renewable energy. When electricity is required, the water is released from the area of high elevation. As it flows downwards, it generates electricity by passing through and rotating a turbine. The second method is to store renewable-generated electricity in specialized lithium ion batteries. The third method is molten salt storage, in which salt is heated to high temperatures using renewable energy and stored in an insulated tank. This high-temperature molten salt can be used to boil water and produce super-heated steam, which can be used to produce electricity on demand. Although a California-based company has successfully installed a molten salt storage system in Nevada, overall the technology is still far from commercialization, so we won't discuss it further here.[131]

With a population of 10,000, El Hierro, an island located in the westernmost part of Spain's Canary Islands, used to be completely dependent on imported diesel for its electricity needs. El Hierro consumed 40,000 barrels of diesel and emitted 18,700 tonnes of $CO_2$ each year. In 2014, to reduce its carbon footprint and reduce reliance on diesel imports, the island installed five 2.3-megawatt wind turbines.[132] To store electricity, the island created a hydropower storage system with an upper reservoir at 715 metres above sea level and a lower reservoir at about 55 metres above sea level. El Hierro now produces a great deal of its electricity from renewable sources, with diesel as a backup, providing an example of how to effectively store renewable energy power.

Yet it's well known that storing electricity using the water elevation method isn't possible everywhere. The most suitable place for this kind of storage is a city or village located in the plains and surrounded by high mountains. Large parts of India, China, the United States and other parts of the world don't have such suitable locations. Moreover, in water-scarce areas of many parts of the world, pumping up the little available water won't be feasible or socially acceptable.

Lithium ion batteries, along with a few other technologies, are now being considered as a serious option in areas where hydropower storage systems don't work. However, the technology isn't perfect yet. Professor Jay Whitacre, an energy storage expert who teaches at Carnegie Mellon University, has highlighted three main challenges with lithium ion batteries: safety, cost and performance.[133]

Some large battery-storage projects have come online across the world in recent years. Yet while many countries are generating renewable electricity to the tune of several gigawatts, battery development is still at the megawatt stage. For example, in February 2017, Californian utility company San Diego Gas & Electric unveiled what it claims is the world's largest lithium ion battery storage facility. Made up of 400,000 batteries, the 30-megawatt facility can store enough energy to serve 20,000 customers for four hours.[134]

Overall, though many companies are working on battery development, the deployment of sufficiently large-scale batteries for storing renewable energy is still some time away. Here's one way to think about it. Suppose you are hosting a big Indian wedding, and you want to give your 1,000 guests ice cream for dessert. The biggest freezer available in town to store ice cream can only fit enough ice cream for 30 guests. But if you don't store the ice cream, it will melt. This is similar to the storage problem renewables are facing today – there isn't enough storage space for later use.

While storage is important, it isn't the only way to manage the intermittency of non-dispatchable renewable energy sources like solar and wind, whose electricity production depends upon factors like time of day and meteorological conditions. Other renewables such as hydro, biomass and geothermal are dispatchable renewables, which means they are ready for production on demand.[135] These renewables can be used in tandem with solar and wind and can be used when the sun isn't shining or the wind isn't blowing. This means that creating an interconnected grid between electricity-producing markets could be one important way of ensuring that electricity is always available for everyone in a renewable energy world.

On the grid transmission and distribution challenges, Vaclav said, "Transition to a renewable energy society is easy for countries like Denmark. They need less electricity, so when wind doesn't blow they can buy electricity from Germany or Sweden. You cannot do this in the US or India or Canada.

The grid connectivity is poor and the various grids are not connected."

Of course, this would also require dealing with current problems that exist with introducing renewables to the grid. Renewables can make the grid unstable – it isn't easy to predict the amount of electricity produced by wind and solar; thus, if they produce too much, or too little, it can lead to brownouts or blackouts (power reductions or power failures). In Germany, one of the most advanced renewable energy markets, grid operators still have to operate conventional fossil-fuel-based power plants in order to stabilize the grid.

The takeaway from all of this for us was that a transition is happening. Governments, companies, civil society organizations, communities and citizens are interested, and a lot of technological development is under way in this area. However, the pace of transition is uncertain, and there are very significant hurdles that have to be overcome if the world is going to transition to 100 per cent renewable energy. Academics like Vaclav point out that historical energy transitions have always happened slowly. In a 2014 article for *Scientific American*, Vaclav wrote, "In the U.S. and around the world, each widespread transition from one dominant fuel to another has taken 50 to 60 years. First came a change from wood to coal. Then from coal to oil. The U.S. is going through a third major energy transition right now, from coal and oil to natural gas."

However, the global climate crisis places unprecedented pressure on national governments. Therefore, the speed at which a transition to renewables will occur remains uncertain. The good news is that we're at the front end of this necessary transition – and have a big opportunity. There's still time to plan effectively for a better future, both for the planet and for the people, if we put our minds to it.

*Chapter Ten*

---

# CREATING THE FUTURE

*Suppose there is a man living by the river in a fire zone. He has children, and belongings. He doesn't want to lose things when fire comes. What should he do? He should build the bridge before fire comes. That's what is required. Similarly, countries have to plan a transition. Give training, and deploy fossil fuel workers in other industries. Create jobs before the transition.*

—Ken Smith, oil sands worker and president of Unifor Local
707-A, a union operating in the Fort McMurray oil sands

Standing in Golakd *basti*, in the middle of the Jharia coalfields, we asked Suresh Bhuiyan whether he would be interested in getting training and working for the solar or wind industry and becoming part of the global shift towards renewables. He nodded his head emphatically. "*Mein jaroor kaam seekhna aur karna chahunga* solar sector *mein* – I will definitely be interested in learning the work and working in the solar sector," he told us. "I have always worked in the coal industry, which is the hardest – I would find other industries easy to work in. But right now the coal industry is my only option for survival."

A few weeks later, thousands of kilometres away in the Canadian oil sands, we asked Robert Grandjambe a similar question – would he be interested in working in the renewable energy sector in the future? "Absolutely," he told us. "If a renewable sector came about, and crushed the oil sands and coal-fired power plants and ideas for nuclear, and we got into wind and solar, and hydro that is built in such a way that it doesn't devastate and eliminate the downstream environment, I will definitely be on board, on so many levels. We have to make a transition to more renewable energy sources. But we also have to change our lifestyle, and be more efficient – using less water and less space. We have to reduce our needs. We can't continue living the way we are living."

Both Suresh and Robert were interested in working in the renewable energy sector. Yet when we started to think about the world transitioning away from its dependency on fossil fuels towards renewable energy, we wondered what would happen to workers like Suresh and Robert. We knew that right now, over 13 million people are directly dependent on fossil fuels for their bread and butter.[136] And, as we saw in Fort McMurray and the coal belt in Jharkhand, businesses and even whole towns have developed to support these industries, generating many jobs. We wondered what would happen to workers, and to entire areas – such as Jharia and Fort McMurray – that revolve around fossil fuel extraction, if an energy transition to renewables occurs. Will people manage to find jobs in the renewable energy industry or other industries? Will they require retraining? Will loss of employment lead to migration and abandonment of existing communities? And, overall, will people's lives become better, worse or simply different?

We also thought about what Robert said – that we can't continue living the way we're living. In a renewable energy future, will it be possible to have it all – to continue enjoying lifestyles that often involve massive consumption? Will renewables seamlessly replace fossil fuel energy? And what about all the petroleum-derived products we enjoy today – rain jackets, yoga pants, plastic containers and more? We wondered what other elements of a transition would look like. Will we have to fundamentally change the way we live and consume, and will people be willing to make those sacrifices?

When we visited T'Sou-ke First Nation in British Columbia, we stayed with Savannah's family. Sandeep had been floored by how many appliances and machines her family used in their everyday lives for tasks that usually were done by hand in his part of India. Some items, such as dishwashers, clothes driers and electric toothbrushes, were uncommon in India but he'd heard of them. Others he'd never imagined anyone would need – like a leaf blower.

Several months later, during our thesis research in the United States, we stayed at the home of one of our colleagues. One of his parents left a slow cooker on the counter to cook chilli during the day, which we would eat that evening. "What's that?" Sandeep asked, staring at the slow cooker bubbling away on the counter. When he found out, he couldn't stop laughing. "You could never have anything like that in Ranchi," he said. "I can't believe the number of machines North Americans use... and some plugged in all day! If you use that in Ranchi, when the power goes out, say goodbye to dinner!" Some of Sandeep's observations might point to reasons why, according to the Global Footprint Network, an international think tank, we would need 4.7 Earths if the world's population lived like Canadians.[137]

◆

We posed our employment questions to Vaclav Smil, the energy transitions expert, during our phone interview with him. As soon as we asked him what he thought would happen to people and communities if an energy transition to renewables occurs, he jumped into answering. "They'll become unemployed, miserable and unhappy. It's a sad story," he told us. "No renewable energies employ people."

We looked at each other. Vaclav was pointing out one of our greatest worries about the transition. We told Vaclav that, by writing our book, we were hoping to raise awareness about the need to plan for transitions for people currently involved in the fossil fuel industry. He told us, "You should write about it. Nobody is paying attention. These are marginal people. They were only good enough to build the Western world with their sweat and tears. Their electricity and energy built these big cities and big industries, and now we don't need them because we buy cheaply from offshore."

Historical evidence supports Vaclav's claims. While writing this book, we read about the impacts of dying industries on individuals and communities dependent on those industries. The UK's coal industry, which had played a huge role in the spread of coal as a source of thermal electricity, employed one million people in 1913. In 1947, when coal was nationalized, it employed approximately 750,000 people. Then, due to the discovery of new sources of energy such as natural gas in the North Sea, and a policy shift favouring the import of coal rather than domestic production, the production of domestic coal declined drastically. By 1994, the entire coal industry in the UK employed just 8,518 people. Experts estimate that 216,000 lost their jobs in the ten-year period between 1984 and 1994.[138] In 2015, the UK closed the last deep coal mine, and the UK coal industry ceased to employ anyone at all. The closure of coal mines had devastating effects on the laid-off workers and their families.[139] Some remained unemployed, while others were forced to migrate in search of work.

*The Economist*, in a 2015 article about the UK coal industry, describes how villagers across Wales and northern England became unemployed and fell to drug use and delinquency when mines were closed in the 1980s. The article states that "tight local culture, based on shared endeavour, village cricket and the miners' social club" also disappeared. Vaclav, during our interview, argued that there is a connection between the end of the coal industry in the UK and the reason that so many people voted for the country's withdrawal from the European Union (EU) during the 2016 UK referendum. "About 80 per cent of the people who voted for UK to leave EU are exactly from former coal mining areas such as Durham and Yorkshire," he said. It was an eye-opener for us. "Policy-makers easily forget about millions of people," he added. It's clear that there hasn't always been enough planning in the past for the transition of the "old" industry as people move to the new.

Ken Smith, the oil sands worker and labour leader we met in Fort McMurray, told us a similar, personal story. Prior to coming to the oil sands, he'd worked for 33 years in a zinc mine in northeastern New Brunswick, Canada. When the mine closed after running out of ore, he along with many others were forced to migrate in search of work. The reason? He states that there was no transition plan for the community, and after the mine closed, there were no other jobs available – despite the fact that everyone knew the closure was coming. "We all knew ten years in advance that they were shutting it down," he told us. "But there were no new industries created in the city at all – zero. Today, unemployment is high. That community is devastated." It didn't have to be that way, he told us. "There was lots of time. There were lots of skilled tradespeople."

He worries about the oil sands. "Fort McMurray was built on oil. It's a small city with a huge population. It's going to die if the oil is done. We're getting a snapshot of it now. The oil prices went down, and now these streets look abandoned. Just some small players couldn't start their projects, and now these streets look abandoned." He shook his head. "If bigger players were to close down in the future, then we'd have a serious problem. We have some very young people doing jobs here. Their future would be doomed."

Such examples can be found the world over. In India, in 2002, when the fertilizer industry shut down in Sindri, a town next to Jharia, thousands of workers lost their jobs. The only help available to them was a government-sponsored "voluntary separation scheme" that essentially provided them with money already owed to them by the government. The laid-off workers, along with the whole town, suffered economically. Even today, the former employees are still demanding their dues from the government.

While some of the stories we've encountered about employment transition are pessimistic, others are more optimistic. And it's hard to know where the future lies. Take, for example, the increasing number of claims that have emerged about green job creation in recent years. These claims state that, globally, the renewable energy industry will generate a huge number of jobs – potentially more than the fossil fuel industry. Dr. Stephan Singer, the director of global energy policy for World Wildlife Fund, wrote in a 2015 blog post that renewables create approximately "three to six times more jobs for the same amount of energy produced than fossil fuels or nuclear." Referring to a recent International Renewable Energy Agency report, he states that renewables, including hydro, employ approximately 9.2 million people worldwide. However, coal and oil and gas only employ a cumulative 13 million people (though, he says, perhaps the numbers are lower – these are industry estimates), despite the fact that they provide ten times more energy than all renewables, including large hydro. He gives the example that solar and wind already employ about four million people across the world while supplying only 5 per cent of global electricity.[140]

Singer does note that not all these jobs are easily transferable – he states, "Staff benefitting from renewable energy expansion are often highly skilled, urban and flexible. That is very different from a coal miner or a gas pipeline worker. One does not make an offshore oil driller in the Gulf of Mexico into a solar PV engineer in San Francisco." He calls for a "just transition" that will involve support for trade unions and workers in this "third industrial revolution," which will involve re-skilling, training and compensation for job losses.

On the other hand, researchers such as Vaclav argue that the renewable energy industry will employ fewer people than the fossil fuel industry. He told us that when comparing employment in the fossil fuel industry and renewables, "You are not even talking apples and oranges, you are talking animals and stars! No way are you going to retrain 10,000 miners to run – what, a PV plant?"

"People always forget the scale," he added. "Even though we have mechanized mining, it still remains a fairly labour-intensive industry. PVs and wind turbines are not labour-intensive at any stage – they are made by machines, erected by machines and run by machines except for maintenance. Hydro is extremely labour-intensive for building it, but later you can run [it] with very few people." He paused for a moment and then added, "China is mining four billion tonnes of coal – you have millions of miners. Half of Chinese coal comes from small mines. No way these millions of people can be retained in the renewable sector. People don't realize what trouble we are in."

Clearly, the claims and opinions conflict. However, it seems clear that in any large-scale change such as this, there will be job winners and losers. The question is how many winners, and how many losers; who will be affected most, and how to help them transition. This is especially important because, even if there are many renewable jobs, it's not clear if people will be able to easily transition from their particular fossil fuel jobs to jobs in the renewable sector or other industries.

As Evan Mills at the University of California wrote in a 2016 article about jobs and off-grid lighting, "In retrospect, few would regret the loss of employment among those who cared for horses following the advent of the car. However, such job displacement should be understood and mitigated to the full extent possible."[141]

As the transition to renewables speeds up, governments will have to seriously think about what will happen to people working in the fossil fuel industry. And when governments start planning for national renewable energy transitions, it is important that they are clear about new job creation (in renewables or any other sector) and how to rehabilitate fossil fuel workers and connected communities.

Ken Smith of Unifor explained the need for governments to have a just transition plan. "Suppose there is a man living by the river in a fire zone. He has children and belongings. He doesn't want to lose things when fire comes. What should he do? He should build the bridge before fire comes. That's what is required. Similarly, countries have to plan a transition. Give training, and deploy fossil fuel workers in other industries. Create jobs before the transition."

Sandeep asked Ken whether he thinks oil sands workers

need a transition plan. He replied, "Yes, absolutely. There are all kinds of things that can be done. There is lots for all of us in Canada. The future doesn't have to be so gloomy. But we have to plan a transition for workers. I was unemployed so I had to move here. But I moved away from my family. Now Fort McMurray is my home and people here are my family members. It's like a temporary community. However, it can't just work on oil. We need to diversify, get training and develop industries like wind, solar and hydro. This will prevent a collapse." Ken is not alone. Many other Canadian trade unions are talking about the just transition, along with policy research institutes and non-profit organizations. Throughout India, let alone in Jharia, there is little discussion about it, and even scantier action.

The idea of a just transition has recently started to attract global attention and is being championed by the International Labour Organization (ILO) and the United Nations Framework Convention on Climate Change (UNFCCC). Just transition was an element in the Paris Agreement, which recognizes "the imperative of a just transition of the workforce and the creation of decent work and quality jobs in accordance with nationally defined development priorities."[142] Since then, the ILO has set out *Guidelines for a Just Transition towards Environmentally Sustainable Economies and Societies for All* and has agreed to team up with the UNFCCC to help boost global action on just transition.[143]

A few global examples of just transition in practice are coming to the forefront. Following the decline of the coal industry in Germany, some German cities have shown examples of a way forward for former coal communities. Essen, in western Germany, has converted old coal mine sites into cultural hubs by creating industrial heritage museums. Each year, millions of tourists visit the Zollverein Coal Mine in Essen, which was designated a UNESCO World Heritage Site in 2001. In this area, local coal communities have transformed and reinvented themselves with the help of government, unions and other stakeholders to ensure a sustainable future.[144] This could be one way of helping fossil-fuel-dependent communities transition to a better future.

China and India have also taken some initiative to transform former coal mines. In Liulong, in east-central Anhui province, China has built a huge floating solar project on a lake that covers a now-abandoned coal mine, and the provincial government has plans to expand this project to at least a dozen more sites. The project employs former coal mining workers from the region, including 57-year-old Yang Xuancheng, who described his switch in professions in an interview for a *New York Times* article: "This aboveground work is so much more pleasant than the hot air down in a coal mine," he said.[145]

In India, local governments are mulling over different options to reorient former fossil fuel workers and their communities. Although these initiatives are still at a preliminary planning stage, they are noteworthy developments. In the Ramgarh district of Jharkhand, about 130 kilometres from Jharia, the local fisheries department is trying to convert mined-out coal mines into lakes and encourage villagers, including former coal industry workers, to form cooperatives and take up fish farming as a new profession.[146]

Ramgarh is a local initiative; there are others at the national level. In 2015, the federal government passed legislation requiring each mining district in the country to set up a District Mineral Foundation (DMF), an agency with a mandate to help communities living in mining areas by empowering them and improving their economic situation. "It took us about seven to eight years to convince the government," explained Chandra Bhushan of the Centre for Science and Environment. "The DMFs are responsible for collecting 10 to 30 per cent of the royalty paid by mining companies, and will also be responsible for using those funds to help the people living in those areas. The funds are meant to be used for educating people, improving health services and improving nutrition. A part of the money should also be kept as funds for the future. I think some of this money could be used for the just transition." One of the key recommendations of the Centre for Science and Environment is that DMF funds should be used "to revive the economy of the area when mining finishes, to avoid the issue of 'ghost towns.'"[147]

Finally, there are some interesting preliminary developments in Alberta. In November 2015, the provincial government announced the introduction of a new Climate Leadership Plan. The plan introduced sweeping changes to Alberta's electricity sector, including the phase-out of coal-generated electricity by 2030.[148] The plan also included the implementation of a new carbon price on greenhouse gas emissions, efforts to develop more renewable energy, a 100-megatonne cap on oil sands emissions and deep reductions in methane emissions.[149]

Phasing out coal-generated electricity by 2030 means hastening the closure of Alberta's coal-fired power plants and associated coal mining and processing operations, affecting over 3,000 workers.[150] In order to help this phase-out process progress smoothly, the provincial government created an Advisory Panel on Coal Communities that met with affected communities, such as Hanna, Alberta, that face large-scale job loss because of the plan.[151] The panel submitted recommendations to the government with advice and options regarding how to support affected workers and communities. The government has also earmarked $998 million from the carbon levy for "large scale renewable energy, bioenergy and technology, coal community transition and other Climate Leadership Plan implementation initiatives," and the Pembina Institute calculated that the government's plans for fostering renewable energy development and energy efficiency in Alberta could generate more jobs than those lost by retiring coal power.[152] As these plans are still very much in the development phase, it remains to be seen how exactly government will help affected workers and communities transition.

All stakeholders need to think about helping making this transition happen. Several of the people we interviewed are already talking about helping fossil fuel workers make a transition to the renewable energy industry. They think that some fossil fuel industry workers could be trained to acquire new skills relevant to the renewable energy industry, which would not only sustain their families but also help the world move towards renewable energy faster.

When we interviewed Jay Bueckert, the Fort McMurray regional director of the Christian Labour Association of Canada, which primarily represents construction and maintenance workers in the oil sands, we asked him about his views on the oil sands industry – and whether he thinks we need a transition to renewable energy. "I think that there's no question we need a transition," he told us unequivocally. "We need to transition to a renewable form of energy that won't have the same impact that oil does."

However, he added, "At the same time, we need to figure out a way to make that transition and still keep people employed so that families can put food on the table." He told us that the reality is you don't need as many workers to put up a wind farm, nor do you need the diverse skill sets found in the oil sands.

"For oil-sands-related projects, you need people that are pipefitters, that are millwrights, that are boilermakers, that are welders – you need a whole host of skill sets. To put up a wind farm you only need someone who can do some civil work – make a concrete pad – and then some folks to be able to hook up these massive wind turbines, so it's just not the same," he told us. He paused and added thoughtfully, "On the flip side – if we're just looking at wind, I don't think that would put everybody to work. But if you're looking at wind, plus hydro, plus solar, plus nuclear, plus all these things, that could do it. We have a really strong workforce, as far as their skill set goes, that could get involved in all of those, that is ready to step into that gap and start working."

Terry Abel of CAPP seconded Bueckert's thoughts. When we asked him whether he thought oil sands workers could be retrained in renewable energy jobs, he said, "I think the simple answer is absolutely yes. One of the hallmarks again of this industry is these are highly skilled workers. Whether they are highly skilled in the different trades associated with constructing and operating these facilities, or they are engineers, scientists, geologists etc., these are very well educated, very skilled people who in my opinion can absolutely transition to other industries and other jobs."

We had heard similar perspectives in India. "See, there would be plenty of options for people currently working in the fossil fuel industry," Ashok Agarwal of the Save Jharia Coalfield Committee told us. "Right now, many people are scavenging coal for survival. People should be trained in new jobs and if possible in renewable energy jobs," he said. "A job transition should be planned properly by the government and all other stakeholders."

Although laid-off fossil fuel workers don't necessarily have to find work in the renewable industry (in the oil sands slump, some former workers started restaurants or went back to school, for example), a few individuals and organizations see an opportunity and have started helping ex-fossil-fuel-industry workers transition towards renewable jobs. One example is Goldwind Americas, an arm of leading Chinese wind turbine manufacturer Goldwind. Intent on expanding its wind farm business into the state of Wyoming, the company has adopted a unique strategy: it is offering a free wind farm technician training program called Goldwind Works, hoping it will attract out-of-work coal mining workers in the state, as well as unemployed workers from other industries. The company envisions these individuals forming part of the hundreds-strong workforce needed to maintain and operate new wind farm projects, such as one the company plans to open in Carbon County, Wyoming.[153]

Lliam Hildebrand, a former oil sands worker, is one of the individuals with vision. In the spring of 2015, amidst plummeting oil prices, he founded a unique non-profit organization called Iron & Earth that helps fossil fuel industry workers transition to work in the renewable energy industry. One of Iron & Earth's most notable initiatives is the Solar Skills program, which aims to retrain 1,000 out-of-work or underemployed energy workers from the oil, gas and coal industries in renewable energy installations and retrofitting. Iron & Earth says workers will be trained in a diverse set of skills, including "high efficiency retrofitting and how to install photovoltaic solar panels, solar heatings and electric vehicle charging stations." Lliam says that the best part is that trainees will learn while building clean-tech infrastructure on high schools in or close to trainees' communities.[154]

During the summer of 2016, when we met Lliam in a coffee shop in Victoria, British Columbia, he was busy getting Iron & Earth's ambitious programs off the ground. The story he told us about why he started Iron & Earth was incredibly inspiring. Before he started to work in the oil sands, he had a moment where he realized that his skills could either create the future or destroy the planet. After high school, he started a steel fabricating apprenticeship in British Columbia, and learned to build all sorts of things – large ship loaders, industrial composters, drilling rigs and more. At a certain point, he started working on a wind farm weather station. "As I was building this structure, I got really interested and started looking more into it. At the same time, I saw Al Gore's documentary *An Inconvenient Truth*. I remember going into the shop the next day and, literally, on one side of the shop, there was the wind farm weather station that I was working on. And on the other side of the shop, not even 20 metres away, we were building pressure vessels for the oil sands," he said.

"I told myself, my trade is the exact skill set that is either going to create the future or destroy the planet through global warming and the carbon-based industry," he said. "That was the moment that really set me on a path to try to figure out how my trade could be the solution and not the problem." Lliam eventually launched his organization in the spring of

2015. He told us, "When oil prices started to fall, we were losing work. My conversations with other colleagues were then centred on incorporating more renewable energy projects into our work scope." Through such conversations, Lliam realized that many of his colleagues in the oil sands believed in climate change and were concerned about the future. Lliam told us that a lot of them realize they are compromising the future of their children's environment. "But what do you do – do you address the current demand for keeping your family alive, or address the future demand for keeping your family alive?"

Sandeep asked Lliam about his vision for Iron & Earth. "I want to see the world reach net zero by 2050," Lliam said. "And I see things going further than that. I think we will get to 100 per cent renewable energy by 2100. And we are going to be living in a completely different world. Within that, I want to see Iron & Earth play an important role in helping thousands of fossil fuel workers transition into renewable energy jobs. I want our organization to help transform the conversation around energy issues and I hope that four years from now it is a very obsolete argument to argue against renewable energy technologies."

He added, "Eventually I would love to start Iron & Earth Industries." He imagines starting a social enterprise or co-op owned and operated by former fossil fuel industry workers that "provides contracting services for large renewable energy projects, and maybe even manufacturing for renewable energy projects."

◆

"I'll never forget Andrew's story," Savannah said as we pushed through the doors of Central European University's new building in downtown Budapest. It was June 2017, and we were about to graduate from our two-year master's program. We reached the Danube River, a five-minute walk away, and sat down on the banks.

"Actually, I think that's how we should end the book," said Sandeep.

Thinking back to our visit to T'Sou-ke First Nation, we remembered the story. Sitting inside the Fisheries building, around a low wooden table, Andrew began to tell us about the T'Sou-ke First Nation's work with children who visited to learn about its environmental initiatives. "You don't want to scare them," he told us. "But on the other hand, they need to feel powerful too. So what we do is we read them a really nice story. I'm sure you know it – the starfish story." He leaned back in his chair and smiled.

"There's this boy walking on the beach after a storm. And the storm has thrown all these starfish up beyond the high-tide line. And there are hundreds of them – and the next tide is not going to catch them. So the little boy starts throwing them into the water. An old man walks by and says, 'Why bother – you'll never be able to make a difference.' The boy pauses, then bends down and picks up a starfish and throws it into the water, then picks up another. 'Well, it made a difference for that one – and this one!'

We all laughed and smiled. Andrew added, "And after we tell them the story, they know they can do something – and they make a challenge tree." He points to the left, where we notice a large green paper tree stuck to the wall covered in small leaf-shaped pieces of paper with children's writing. "Have a look at what's on the leaves," he said.

Savannah walked over and read aloud, "I will take a short shower. And try to use a reusable cup."

"So you end up with a tree full of promises and commitments," Andrew told us. He explained that it's about behaviour change – that we adults already have fixed our habits, but children don't have fixed habits yet and have an immense potential to choose environmentally beneficial ones.

"So that's really it," Andrew told us. "Imagine you're a 5-year-old, and you've started to pick up on the idea of climate change, and you wonder, *What can I do about it?* Well you can have shorter showers. And so on. So these children make a commitment. And they're totally sincere. Which is fabulous to see. And usually they take the challenge tree back to school with them – but they left this one."

"Wow," said Savannah. "So it gives them some personal agency. They can make a commitment that protects them against feeling powerless because of this very scary thing – climate change – that we're all facing. They can say, 'I have some power to take action, and do it, and feel empowered.'"

"Exactly," Andrew replied. "And we use the pester factor. They then go home and pester their parents, 'Mom you've left the lights on again,' and so on," he said. We all laughed. "We're all a bit cynical and stuck in our ways... because since a young age we were stuck in front of a TV, and our unconscious is colonized by Disney. We're waiting for the fairy godmother to appear any minute and wave her wand and make it all right – but I think she's working for the oil companies! They've bought her out! Here we are, waiting for someone else to solve our problems, whereas we can actually start doing something today. And it takes very little – we can take our power back!"

Back in Budapest, Savannah turned to Sandeep. "That story really gave me hope," she said. "It's amazing what they're doing... and Iron & Earth, and Ken Smith and so many others."

"That's true," Sandeep replied. "And it's going to take initiatives like this – from communities, and regular people, and governments, everyone – to make a total transition happen and to make it successful. One where fossil fuel industry workers like Suresh and Robert will have a bright future."

# EPILOGUE

After writing this book, Savannah and Sandeep both graduated from MESPOM and received their master's degrees, with distinction. They moved to British Columbia, where Savannah started an articling position at the University of Victoria's Environmental Law Centre – an important step on her journey to becoming lawyer. Sandeep received the Graduate Global Leadership Fellowship to pursue doctoral studies at the University of British Columbia. He plans to focus his research on the social dimensions of energy transitions.

During their master's research in Kenya, they went to the Maasai Mara National Reserve in southwestern Kenya to enjoy the preserved savannah wilderness. One evening, overlooking the reserve, Sandeep proposed to Savannah, and they decided to spend their lives together. In July 2017, Savannah and Sandeep married in Savannah's family's backyard in Victoria, British Columbia. They remain committed to supporting positive change – for people, communities and the planet.

# NOTES

## PART I: A JOURNEY BEGINS

### CHAPTER ONE: BEGINNINGS IN BUDAPEST

1 Colin P. Kelley et al., "Climate change in the Fertile Crescent and implications of the recent Syrian drought," *PNAS* 112 (2015): 3242, doi:10.1073/pnas.1421533112.

2 Sandeep Pai, "Unrest in parched land," *DNA*, October 23, 2015, http://epaper.dnaindia.com/epapermain.aspx?pgNo=10&edcode=820009&eddate=2015-10-23.

### CHAPTER TWO: HOOKED ON FOSSIL FUELS

3 European Commission, *Towards an Energy Union: Hungary* (Brussels: European Union, 2015), 2, https://www.parlament.gv.at/PAKT/EU/XXV/EU/08/46/EU_84628/imfname_10590332.pdf.

4 Vaclav Smil, *Energy: A Beginner's Guide* (Oxford: Oneworld Publications, 2006), 7–9.

5 BP, *BP Statistical Review of World Energy June 2016* (UK: Pureprint, 2016), 41, https://www.bp.com/content/dam/bp/pdf/energy-economics/statistical-review-2016/bp-statistical-review-of-world-energy-2016-full-report.pdf.

6 "U.S. Energy Facts Explained," US Energy Information Administration, http://www.eia.gov/energyexplained/?page=us_energy_home.

7 United States of America Department of Energy, *U.S. Energy and Employment Report: January 2017*, 8, https://www.energy.gov/sites/prod/files/2017/01/f34/2017%20US%20Energy%20and%20Jobs%20Report_0.pdf.

8 BP, *BP Statistical Review*, 41.

9 Zongyun Song, Dongxiao Niu and Xinli Xiao, "Focus on the current competitiveness of coal industry in China: Has the depression time gone?" *Resources Policy* 51 (2017): 173, doi:10.1016/j.resourpol.2016.11.011.

10 BP, *BP Statistical Review*, 41.

11 Ibid.

12 Sandeep Pai and Bilal Handoo, "Coal India raises doubts about its future," *Nikkei Asian Review*, January 31, 2017, http://asia.nikkei.com/Business/AC/Coal-India-raises-doubts-about-its-future?page=2.

13 BP, *BP Statistical Review*, 41.

14 "Canadian Economic Contribution," Canadian Association of Petroleum

Producers, http://www.capp.ca/canadian-oil-and-natural-gas/canadian-economic-contribution.

15 Edward Wong, "Coal Burning Causes the Most Air Pollution Deaths in China, Study Finds," *The New York Times*, August 17, 2016, https://www.nytimes.com/2016/08/18/world/asia/china-coal-health-smog-pollution.html?_r=o.

16 Sarah Graham, "Environmental Effects of *Exxon Valdez* Spill Still Being Felt," *Scientific American*, December 19, 2003, https://www.scientificamerican.com/article/environmental-effects-of/.

17 Natural Resources Defense Council, *Summary of Information concerning the Ecological and Economic Impacts of the BP Deepwater Horizon Oil Spill Disaster*, https://www.nrdc.org/sites/default/files/gulfspill-impacts-summary-IP.pdf; Riannon Westall, "BP oil spill: The economic and environmental cost, 5 years later," CBC News, April 17, 2015, http://www.cbc.ca/news/multimedia/bp-oil-spill-the-economic-and-environmental-cost-5-years-later-1.3037553.

18 NASA, "A blanket around the Earth," http://climate.nasa.gov/causes/.

19 Ibid.

20 Intergovernmental Panel on Climate Change, *Climate Change 2014 Synthesis Report: Summary for Policymakers* (Geneva, Switzerland: IPCC, 2014), 5, http://www.ipcc.ch/pdf/assessment-report/ar5/syr/AR5_SYR_FINAL_SPM.pdf.

21 NASA, "Blanket around the Earth."

22 Intergovernmental Panel on Climate Change, *Climate Change 2014 Synthesis Report*, 2, 8; "The Carbon Budget," World Resources Institute, http://www.wri.org/sites/default/files/WRI13-IPCCinfographic-FINAL_web.png.

23 Robin McKie, "Scientists warn world will miss key climate target," *The Guardian*, August 6, 2016, https://www.theguardian.com/science/2016/aug/06/global-warming-target-miss-scientists-warn.

24 Ibid.

25 United Nations, "IPCC Report: 'severe and pervasive' impacts of climate change will be felt everywhere," *United Nations Blog*, March 31, 2014, http://www.un.org/climatechange/blog/2014/03/ipcc-report-severe-and-pervasive-impacts-of-climate-change-will-be-felt-everywhere/.

26 "Climate Change Vulnerability Index 2011," Maplecroft, https://maplecroft.com/about/news/ccvi.html.

27 Edward Wong, "China Poised to Take Lead on Climate After Trump's Move to Undo Policies," *The New York Times*, March 29, 2017, https://www.nytimes.com/2017/03/29/world/asia/trump-climate-change-paris-china.html.

28 Frankfurt School-UNEP Centre/BNEF, *Global Trends in Renewable Energy Investment 2016*, 11, http://fs-unepcentre.org/sites/default/files/publications/globaltrendsinrenewableenergyinvestment2016lowres_0.pdf.

29 Vaclav Smil, *Energy Transitions: History, Requirements, Prospects* (Santa Barbara: Praeger, 2010), chap. 3. Kindle edition.

30 Roger Fouquet and Peter Pearson, "Past and prospective energy transitions: insights from history," *Energy Policy* 50 (2012): 1, doi:10.1016/j.enpol.2012.08.014.

31 Smil, *Energy Transitions*, chap. 3.

32 Andreas Malm, *Fossil Capital: The Rise of Steam Power and the Roots of Global Warming* (London: Verso, 2016), chap. 1. Kindle edition.

33 BBC News, "History," http://www.bbc.co.uk/history/historic_figures/watt_james.shtml.

34 Malm, *Fossil Capital*, chap. 1.

35 Patricia Crone, *Pre-Industrial Societies: Anatomy of the Pre-Modern World* (London: Oneworld Publications, 2003), chap. 1–chap. 2. Kindle edition.

36 Tony Seba, *Clean Disruption of Energy and Transportation* (US: Tony Seba, 2014), 49–50.

37 Ibid., 3.

## PART II: JOURNEY TO JHARKHAND

### CHAPTER THREE: THE COAL-CYCLE *WALLAH*

38 Coal India Limited, *Annual Report 2015-2016: Chapter 11 Safety in Coal Mines*, http://coal.nic.in/sites/upload_files/coal/files/coalupload/chap11AnnualReport1516en.pdf.

39 DNA Correspondent, "Every 24 hours a coal miner dies in India, but who cares," *DNA*, September 21, 2011, http://www.dnaindia.com/mumbai/report-dna-investigations-every-24-hours-a-coal-miner-dies-in-india-but-who-cares-1589657.

40 The standing committee on safety in coal mines (New Delhi), "Minutes of the meeting of the standing committee on safety in coal mines 13 March 2015," http://coal.nic.in/sites/upload_files/coal/files/curentnotices/agenda feb172016.PDF.

41 Anumeha Yadav, "Jharkhand disaster: Miners say they warned bosses of imminent danger but were ordered back to work," *Scroll.in*, January 19, 2017, https://scroll.in/article/826673/jharkhand-coal-mine-workers-say-they-warned-of-imminent-danger-that-eventually-left-23-dead.

42 India Ministry of Coal, "Coal Reserves," http://coal.nic.in/content/coal-reserves.

43 Press Information Bureau, Government of India, "CIL Gearing Up For 1 Billion Tonne Coal Production Mark," http://pib.nic.in/newsite/PrintRelease.aspx?relid=115635.

44 Leen Abdallah, "The Cost to End World Hunger," *The Borgen Project Blog*,

February 15, 2013, https://borgenproject.org/the-cost-to-end-world
-hunger/; Victor Mallet and James Crabtree, "Coal deal lost India
$33-billion, says auditor," *The Globe and Mail*, August 17, 2012, http://www
.theglobeandmail.com/report-on-business/international-business
/asian-pacific-business/coal-deal-lost-india-33-billion-says-auditor
/article4486464/.

45 Sandeep Pai and Gangadhar Patil, "Revealed: How Coal India flouted
Environment Ministry guidelines," DNA, January 4, 2012, http://
www.dnaindia.com/india/report-revealed-how-coal-india-flouted
-environment-ministry-guidelines-1633244.

46 Avishek Rakshit, "Jharkhand revises royalty income from coal auctions,"
*Business Standard*, August 19, 2016, http://www.business-standard.com
/article/economy-policy/jharkhand-revises-royalty-income-from-coal
-auctions-116081901422_1.html.

47 Glenn B. Stracher and Tammy P. Taylor, "The Global Catastrophe," in
*Coal and Peat Fires: A Global Perspective: Volume 1: Coal—Geology and
Combustion*, eds. Glenn B. Stracher, Anupma Prakash and Ellina V. Sokol
(Amsterdam: Elsevier, 2011), 101–102.

## CHAPTER FOUR: DANTE'S INFERNO, EASTERN INDIA

48 Jitendra Pandey et al., "Environmental and socio-economic impacts of
fire in Jharia coalfield, Jharkhand, India: an appraisal," *Current Science*
110 (2016): 1641, doi:10.18520/cs/v110/i9/1639–50.

49 Varinder Saini, Ravi P. Gupta and Manoj K. Arora, "Environmental impact studies in coalfields in India: A case study from Jharia coal-field,"
*Renewable and Sustainable Energy Reviews* 53 (2016): 1230, doi:10.1016/j
.rser.2015.09.072.

50 "Jharia Master Plan," Bharat Coking Coal Limited, http://www.bcclweb
.in/?page_id=25902.

51 Pandey et al., "Impacts of fire in Jharia," 1640.

52 Bhanu Pandey, Madhoolika Agrawal and Siddharth Singh, "Assessment
of air pollution around coal mining area: Emphasizing on spatial distributions, seasonal variations and heavy metals, using cluster and
principal component analysis," *Atmospheric Pollution Research* 5 (2014):
83, doi:10.5094/APR.2014.010; World Health Organisation, WHO *Air
quality guidelines for particulate matter, ozone, nitrogen dioxide and sul-
fur dioxide*, http://apps.who.int/iris/bitstream/10665/69477/1/WHO_
SDE_PHE_OEH_06.02_eng.pdf.

53 Pandey et al., "Impacts of fire in Jharia," 1645.

# PART III: JOURNEY TO ALBERTA

### CHAPTER SIX: A BLACK GOLD RUSH TOWN

54 Angela Fritz, "Fort McMurray wildfire evacuation was largest on record in Canada," *The Washington Post*, May 4, 2016, https://www.washingtonpost.com/news/capital-weather-gang/wp/2016/05/04/hot-dry-and-windy-weather-stokes-the-violent-alberta-wildfire/.

55 Blair King, "We Can't Blame Climate Change for the Fort McMurray Fires," *The Huffington Post*, October 5, 2016; Henry Fountain, "Dry Winter and Warm Spring Set Stage for Wildfire in Canada," *The New York Times*, May 5, 2016, https://www.nytimes.com/2016/05/06/science/dry-winter-and-warm-spring-set-stage-for-canadian-inferno.html?_r=0.

56 Mike De Souza, "Here's what the science really says about Fort McMurray and climate change," *National Observer*, June 3, 2016, http://www.nationalobserver.com/2016/06/03/analysis/heres-what-science-really-says-about-fort-mcmurray-and-climate-change.

57 Alberta Energy, "What is Oil Sands?" http://www.energy.gov.ab.ca/oilsands/793.asp.

58 Alberta Energy, "Facts and Statistics," http://www.energy.alberta.ca/OilSands/791.asp.

59 Alberta Energy, "Resource," http://www.energy.gov.ab.ca/OilSands/1715.asp.

60 Alberta Energy, "Facts and Statistics."

61 Peter Findlay, *The Future of the Canadian Oil Sands: Growth potential of a unique resource amidst regulation, egress, cost and price uncertainty*, OIES Paper: WPM 64 (Oxford: The University of Oxford, Oxford Institute for Energy Studies, 2016), 24, https://www.oxfordenergy.org/wpcms/wp-content/uploads/2016/02/The-Future-of-the-Canadian-Oil-Sands-WPM-64.pdf.

62 Natural Resources Canada, "Oil Supply and Demand," https://www.nrcan.gc.ca/energy/oil-sands/18086.

63 Morgan Modjeski, "Income Inequality and the Oil Sands: Fort McMurray's Rich 20-Somethings Find Hard Times Hard To Understand," *The Huffington Post*, June 3, 2012, http://www.huffingtonpost.ca/2012/03/05/income-gap-oilsands-fort-mcmurray_n_1321666.html.

64 Tavia Grant and Bill Curry, "The wealth of the nation: A snapshot of what Canadians earn," *The Globe and Mail*, September 11, 2013, http://www.theglobeandmail.com/news/politics/who-are-the-1-per-cent-a-snapshot-of-what-canadians-earn/article14269972/?page=all.

65 Tracy Johnson, "Just how many jobs have been cut in the oilpatch?" CBC News, July 6, 2016, http://www.cbc.ca/news/canada/calgary/oil-patch-layoffs-how-many-1.3665250.

66 CBC News, "Suicide rate in Alberta climbs 30% in wake of mass oilpatch layoffs," December 7, 2015, http://www.cbc.ca/news/canada/calgary /suicide-rate-alberta-increase-layoffs-1.3353662.

67 Justin Giovannetti, "Low oil prices, costly wildfire push Alberta's deficit to nearly $11-billion," *The Globe and Mail*, August 23, 2016, http://www .theglobeandmail.com/news/alberta/fort-mcmurray-wildfire-adds -500-million-to-albertas-projected-deficit/article31515924/.

68 Robson Fletcher, "'Nobody knocks Alberta down for long': Notley aims to reassure anxious Albertans in major speech," CBC News, October 19, 2016, http://www.cbc.ca/news/canada/calgary/notley-state-of-the-province -calgary-setup-1.3810219.

69 Findlay, *Canadian Oil Sands*, 13.

70 Natural Resources Canada, "Oil Sands: GHG Emissions - US," http:// www.nrcan.gc.ca/energy/publications/18731.

71 Sweden Sverige, "SWEDEN TACKLES CLIMATE CHANGE," https://sweden .se/nature/sweden-tackles-climate-change/; "Capping oil sands emis- sions," Alberta Government, https://www.alberta.ca/climate-oilsands -emissions.aspx.

72 Findlay, *Canadian Oil Sands*, 15–16.

73 Claudia Cattaneo, "Fort McKay Chief Jim Boucher explores building the first aboriginal oilsands project: 'Timing is right,'" *Financial Post*, June 27, 2016, http://business.financialpost.com/news/energy/fort-mckay-chief -jim-boucher-explores-building-the-first-aboriginal-oilsands-project -timing-is-right.

74 Fort McKay First Nation, *Business Ventures & Industry Relations*, http:// fortmckay.com/wp-content/uploads/flipbook/2/mobile/index.html.

75 CBC News, "Canadian Natural Resources fined $500,000 for hydro- gen sulphide releases," June 24, 2016, http://www.cbc.ca/news/canada /edmonton/canadian-natural-resources-fined-500-000-for-hydrogen -sulphide-releases-1.3652379.

76 Alberta Energy Regulator and Alberta Health, *Recurrent Human Health Complaints Technical Information Synthesis: Fort McKay Area* (Calgary: Alberta Energy Regulator, 2016), ix, http://aer.ca/documents/reports /FortMcKay_FINAL.pdf.

77 Vincent McDermott, "Study puts spotlight on air quality, odour con- cerns in Fort McKay," *Fort McMurray Today*, September 21, 2016, http:// www.fortmcmurraytoday.com/2016/09/21/study-puts-spotlight -on-air-quality-odour-concerns-in-fort-mckay.

## CHAPTER SEVEN: THE TRAPPER, HUNTER AND MILLWRIGHT

78 Jodi McNeill, "Will Alberta's oilsands tailings finally be cleaned up?" Pembina Institute blog, February 8, 2017, http://www.pembina.org /blog/will-alberta-s-oilsands-tailings-finally-be-cleaned-up.

79 Jodi McNeill, "Oilsands tailings back in the spotlight," Pembina Institute blog, December 5, 2016, http://www.pembina.org/blog /oilsands-tailings-back-spotlight.

80 Josh Wingrove, "Syncrude to pay $3M for duck deaths," *The Globe and Mail*, October 22, 2010, https://www.theglobeandmail.com/report -on-business/industry-news/energy-and-resources/syncrude-to -pay-3m-for-duck-deaths/article4085700/.

81 CBC News, "The Syncrude duck trial," March 25, 2010, http://www.cbc .ca/news/canada/edmonton/the-syncrude-duck-trial-1.873354.

82 CBC News, "Oilsands tailings ponds kill more ducks," October 26, 2010, http://www.cbc.ca/news/canada/edmonton/oilsands-tailings-ponds -kill-more-ducks-1.934577.

83 Richard A. Frank et al., "Profiling Oil Sands Mixtures from Industrial Developments and Natural Groundwaters for Source Identification," *Environmental Science & Technology* 48 (2014): 2660, doi:10.1021/ es500131k; for press coverage of the report, see CBC News, "Oilsands study confirms tailings found in groundwater, river," February 20, 2014, http://www.cbc.ca/news/canada/edmonton/oilsands-study-confirms -tailings-found-in-groundwater-river-1.2545089.

84 "Wood Buffalo National Park," United Nations Educational, Scientific and Cultural Organization, http://whc.unesco.org/en/list/256.

85 "Delta Wildlife," Peace-Athabasca Delta Ecological Monitoring Program, http://www.pademp.com/delta-ecology/wildlife/.

86 Andrew Nikiforuk, "Alberta Health Board Fires Doctor who Raised Cancer Alarms," *The Tyee*, May 11, 2015, https://thetyee.ca/News/2015 /05/11/John-OConnor-Fired/; Alberta Cancer Board Division of Population Health and Information Surveillance, *Cancer Incidence in Fort Chipewyan, Alberta 1995–2006*, 8, http://www.albertahealthservices .ca/rls/ne-rls-2009-02-06-fort-chipewyan-study.pdf.

87 Findlay, *Canadian Oil Sands*, 15–16.

88 Marty Klinkenberg, "Oil sands pollution linked to higher cancer rates in Fort Chipewyan for first time: study," *Financial Post*, July 8, 2014, http://business.financialpost.com/news/oil-sands-pollution-linked-to -higher-cancer-rates-in-fort-chipewyan-study-finds.

89 Mikisew Cree First Nation, "Written Brief of the Mikisew Cree First Nation to the Standing Committee on Environment and Sustainable Development," November 15, 2016, 3–6, http://www.ourcommons.ca /Content/Committee/421/ENVI/Brief/BR8622379/br-external /MikisewCreeFirstNation-e.pdf.

90 David W. Schindler, "Unravelling the complexity of pollution by the oil sands industry," *PNAS* 111 (2014): 3209, doi:10.1073/pnas.1400511111.

91 Erin N. Kelly et al., "Oil sands development contributes polycyclic aromatic compounds to the Athabasca River and its tributaries," *PNAS* 106

(2009): 22346, doi:10.1073/pnas.0912050106; Erin N. Kelly et al., "Oil sands development contributes elements toxic at low concentrations to the Athabasca River and its tributaries," *PNAS* 107 (2010): 16178, doi:10.1073/pnas.1008754107, as cited in Schindler, "Unravelling the complexity," 3209.

92 Schindler, "Unravelling the complexity," 3209.

93 Joshua Kurek et al., "Legacy of a half century of Athabasca oil sands development recorded by lake ecosystems," *PNAS* 110 (2013): 1761, doi:10.1073/pnas.1217675110, as cited in Schindler, "Unravelling the complexity," 3209.

94 Craig E. Hebert et al., "Mercury Trends in Colonial Waterbird Eggs Downstream of the Oil Sands Region of Alberta, Canada," *Environmental Science and Technology* 47 (2013): 11785, 11791, doi:10.1021/es402542w, as cited in Mikisew Cree First Nation, *Petition to the World Heritage Committee Requesting Inclusion of Wood Buffalo National Park on the List of World Heritage in Danger*, 25, http://cpawsnab.org/uploads/Mikisew_Petition_respecting_UNESCO_Site_256_-_December_8,_2014.PDF.

95 "Q&A: Gull and Tern Egg Consumption Advisory," Alberta Government, http://mywildalberta.com/hunting/safety-procedures/documents/QA-Gull-Tern-EggAdvisory-May16-2014.pdf, as cited in Mikisew Cree, *Petition to the World Heritage Committee*, 25.

96 Kevin P. Timoney, *A study of Water and Sediment Quality as Related to Public Health Issues, Fort Chipewyan, Alberta*, on behalf of the Nunee Health Board Society, 63, https://sites.ualberta.ca/~swfc/images/fc-final-report-revised-dec2007.pdf, as cited in Mikisew Cree, *Petition to the World Heritage Committee*, 25–26.

97 Vincent McDermott, "Media-shy Jane Fonda is latest celebrity to visit Alberta oilsands," *Edmonton Journal*, January 10, 2017, http://edmontonjournal.com/news/local-news/media-shy-jane-fonda-is-latest-celebrity-to-visit-alberta-oilsands.

98 United Nations Educational, Scientific and Cultural Organization, "State of Conservation: Wood Buffalo National Park (Canada)," http://whc.unesco.org/en/soc/3318.

99 UNESCO World Heritage Centre and International Union for Conservation of Nature, *Reactive Monitoring Mission to Wood Buffalo National Park, Canada 25 September - 4 October 2016: Mission Report, March 2017*, 38, http://whc.unesco.org/en/documents/156893, as cited in Canadian Press, "In danger: UNESCO issues warning about Wood Buffalo National Park," CBC News, March 10, 2017, http://www.cbc.ca/news/canada/edmonton/unesco-wood-buffalo-national-park-in-danger-conservation-fears-1.4019549.

# PART IV: JOURNEY FORWARD

## CHAPTER EIGHT: THE RENEWABLE REVOLUTION

100 Evan Mills, "Job creation and energy savings through a transition to modern off-grid lighting," *Energy for Sustainable Development* 33 (2016): 155, doi:10.1016/j.esd.2016.06.001.

101 Seba, *Clean Disruption*, 149.

102 Renewable Energy Policy Network for the 21st Century, *Renewables 2016: Global Status Report* (Paris: REN21 Secretariat, 2016), 17, http:// www.ren21.net/wp-content/uploads/2016/06/GSR_2016_Full_Report_ REN21.pdf.

103 United States of America, *Intended nationally determined contribution*, http://www4.unfccc.int/Submissions/INDC/Published%20Documents /United%20States%20of%20America/1/U.S.%20Cover%20Note%20 INDC%20and%20Accompanying%20Information.pdf.

104 Lizzie Dearden, "Angela Merkel calls Donald Trump's Paris withdrawal 'extremely regrettable' in 'very restrained terms,'" *The Independent*, June 2, 2017, http://www.independent.co.uk/news/world/europe/angela-merkel -donald-trump-paris-agreement-withdraw-regrettable-germany -mother-earth-restrained-a7768551.html.

105 We Are Still In Coalition, "We Are Still In," http://wearestillin.com/.

106 "Canada's INDC Submission to the UNFCCC," http://www4.unfccc.int /ndcregistry/PublishedDocuments/Canada%20First/INDC%20-%20 Canada%20-%20English.pdf.

107 Umair Irfan, "Climate Pledges Will Fall Short of Needed 2 Degree C Limit," *Scientific American*, November 3, 2016, https://www.scientificamerican .com/article/climate-pledges-will-fall-short-of-needed-2-degree-c-limit/.

108 Eliza Northrop, "Not Just for Paris, but for the Future: How the Paris Agreement Will Keep Accelerating Climate Action," World Resources Institute blog, December 14, 2015, http://www.wri.org/blog/2015/12 /not-just-paris-future-how-paris-agreement-will-keep-accelerating -climate-action.

109 "IEA raises its five-year renewable growth forecast as 2015 marks record year," International Energy Agency, https://www.iea.org/newsroom /news/2016/october/iea-raises-its-five-year-renewable-growth-forecast -as-2015-marks-record-year.html.

110 Robert Fares, "The Price of Solar Is Declining to Unprecedented Lows," *Plugged In* blog (*Scientific American*), August 27, 2016, https://blogs .scientificamerican.com/plugged-in/the-price-of-solar-is-declining -to-unprecedented-lows/.

111 LeAnne Graves, "Adipec 2016: Low cost of solar may be a loss for gas," *The National*, May 23, 2017, http://www.thenational.ae/business /abu-dhabi-oil/adipec-2016-low-cost-of-solar-may-be-a-loss-for-gas.

112  Jamie Ayque, "Roads of the Future: Solar Highways Becoming a Reality," *Nature World News*, September 23, 2016, http://www.natureworldnews .com/articles/29080/20160923/roads-future-solar-highways-becoming -reality.htm.

113  Rob Davies, "Kite power to take flight in Scotland next year," *The Guardian*, October 7, 2016, https://www.theguardian.com/business/2016/oct/07 /kite-power-solutions-scotland-green-energy.

114  Ibid.

115  Ian Johnston, "One of world's first kite-driven power stations set to open in Scotland," *The Independent*, October 6, 2016, http://www .independent.co.uk/environment/kite-power-station-scotland-wind -turbine-plant-electricity-a7348576.html.

## CHAPTER NINE: LAST HURDLES

116  Vaclav Smil, *Energy Transitions: Global and National Perspectives*, 2nd ed (Santa Barbara, CA: Praeger, 2017), chap. 4

117  Mark Z. Jacobson and Cristina L. Archer, "Saturation wind power potential and its implications for wind energy," PNAS 109 (2007): 15679, doi:10.1073/pnas.1208993109/-/DCSupplemental.

118  US Energy Information Administration, "Use of Energy in the United States Explained," https://www.eia.gov/Energyexplained/?page=us_ energy_transportation.

119  US Environmental Protection Agency, "Global Greenhouse Gas Emissions Data," https://www.epa.gov/ghgemissions/global-greenhouse-gas -emissions-data; Intergovernmental Panel on Climate Change, *Climate Change 2014 Synthesis Report*, 8.

120  Charles Morris, *Tesla Motors: How Elon Musk and Company Made Electric Cars Cool, and Sparked the Next Tech Revolution* (USA: Bluespages, 2014), chap. 2. Kindle Edition.

121  International Energy Agency, *Global EV Outlook 2016: Beyond one million electric cars*, 8, https://www.iea.org/publications/freepublications /publication/Global_EV_Outlook_2016.pdf.

122  Morris, *Tesla Motors*, chap. 1.

123  Damian Carrington, "Solar Impulse 2 completes first ever Atlantic crossing by solar plane," *The Guardian*, June 23, 2016, https://www.theguardian .com/environment/2016/jun/23/solar-impulse-2-completes-first-ever -atlantic-crossing-by-solar-plane.

124  Amar Doshi et al., "Economic and policy issues in the production of algae-based biofuels: A review," *Renewable and Sustainable Energy Reviews* 64 (2016): 330, doi:10.1016/j.rser.2016.06.027.

125  Eva-Mari Aro, "From first generation biofuels to advanced solar biofuels," *Ambio* 45, Suppl. 1 (2016): S25, doi:10.1007/s13280-015-0730-0.

126  D. Leeson et al., "A Techno-economic analysis and systematic review of carbon capture and storage (CCS) applied to the iron and steel, cement, oil refining and pulp and paper industries, as well as other high purity sources," *International Journal of Greenhouse Gas Control* 61 (2017): 73, doi:10.1016/j.ijggc.2017.03.020.

127  Commonwealth Scientific and Industrial Research Organisation, "Environmentally-friendly steelmaking," CSIRO, https://www.csiro.au/en/Research/MRF/Areas/Community-and-environment/Responsible-resource-development/Green-steelmaking; Gill South, "Small business: Clean-tech firm lands NZ Steel deal," *The New Zealand Herald*, February 18, 2013, http://www.nzherald.co.nz/business/news/article.cfm?c_id=3&objectid=10865997.

128  Leeson et al., "A Techno-economic analysis," 75.

129  Vaclav Smil, *Enriching the Earth: Fritz Haber, Carl Bosch, and the Transformation of World Food Production* (Cambridge, MA: Massachusetts Institute of Technology, 2001), 160.

130  K. Hasler et al., "Life cycle assessment (LCA) of different fertilizer product types," *European Journal of Agronomy* 69 (2015): 42, doi:10.1016/j.eja.2015.06.001.

131  Knvul Sheikh, "New Concentrating Solar Tower Is Worth Its Salt with 24/7 Power," *Scientific American*, July 14, 2016, https://www.scientificamerican.com/article/new-concentrating-solar-tower-is-worth-its-salt-with-24-7-power/.

132  Stephan Hülsmann, Atle Harby and Richard Taylor, *The need for water as energy storage for better integration of renewables*, Policy Brief No. 01/2015 (Dresden: United Nations University Institute for the Integrated Management of Material Fluxes and of Resources, 2015), 4, http://programme.worldwaterweek.org/sites/default/files/unu-flores_policy-brief_01-2015.pdf.

133  Jay Whitacre, "3 Challenges: Lithium Ion Battery Safety, Cost, and Performance," *Aquion Energy* blog, September 16, 2016, http://blog.aquionenergy.com/lithium-ion-battery-safety-cost-and-performance-challenges.

134  SDG&E, "SDG&E Unveils World's Largest Lithium Ion Battery Storage Facility," press release, February 28, 2017, http://sdgenews.com/battery-storage/sdge-unveils-world's-largest-lithium-ion-battery-storage-facility.

135  International Energy Agency Energy–Technology Systems Analysis Program and International Renewable Energy Agency, *Renewable Energy Integration in Power Grids: Technology Brief E15– April 2015*, 1, http://www.irena.org/DocumentDownloads/Publications/IRENA-ETSAP_Tech_Brief_Power_Grid_Integration_2015.pdf.

## CHAPTER TEN: CREATING THE FUTURE

136 Stephan Singer, "With 9.2 million employed by renewable energy, is the jobs myth finally bust?" *Climate and Energy* blog (World Wildlife Fund), May 25, 2015, http://climate-energy.blogs.panda.org/2015/05/25/with-9-2-million-employed-by-renewable-energy-is-the-jobs-myth-finally-bust/.

137 "Earth's resources depleted for 2016," World Wildlife Fund, http://www.wwf.ca/?21901/Earths-resources-depleted-for-2016.

138 Emma Hollywood, "Mining, Migration and Immobility: Towards an understanding of the relationship between migration and occupation in the context of the UK mining industry," *International Journal of Population Geography* 8 (2002): 299, doi:10.1002/ijpg.264.

139 BBC News, "Watching the pits disappear," March 5, 2004, http://news.bbc.co.uk/2/hi/uk/3514549.stm.

140 Singer, "With 9.2 million employed."

141 Mills, "Job creation," 155.

142 International Labour Organization, "Decent work and just transitions must be at the heart of climate action," http://www.ilo.org/global/topics/green-jobs/news/WCMS_475064/lang--en/index.htm; United Nations, *Paris Agreement*, 2, http://unfccc.int/files/essential_background/convention/application/pdf/english_paris_agreement.pdf.

143 International Labour Organization, "ILO and UNFCCC team up to boost action on just transition and decent work in the context of climate change," http://www.ilo.org/global/about-the-ilo/newsroom/news/WCMS_547216/lang--en/index.htm?shared_from=media-mail.

144 Nora Löhle, "A just transition: The way forward for coal communities," Heinrich Böll Foundation blog, March 14, 2017, https://www.boell.de/en/2017/03/14/just-transition-way-forward-coal-communities.

145 Keith Bradsher, "China Looks to Capitalize on Clean Energy as U.S. Retreats," *The New York Times*, June 5, 2017, https://mobile.nytimes.com/2017/06/05/business/energy-environment/china-clean-energy-coal-pollution.html?smid=fb-nytimes&smtyp=cur&referer=http%3A%2F%2Fm.facebook.com%2F.

146 *The Times of India*, "Central Coalfields Limited abandoned mines may be used for fish farming," March 3, 2015, http://timesofindia.indiatimes.com/city/ranchi/Central-Coalfields-Limited-abandoned-mines-may-be-used-for-fish-farming/articleshow/46442697.cms.

147 Centre for Science and Environment, *District Mineral Foundation*, http://www.cseindia.org/userfiles/District%20Mineral%20Foundation.pdf.

148 "Climate Leadership Plan," *Alberta Government*, https://www.alberta.ca/climate-leadership-plan.aspx.

149 Ibid.

150 Binnu Jeyakumar, *Job Growth in Clean Energy: Employment in Alberta's emerging renewables and energy efficiency sectors*, Pembina Institute, 8, https://www.pembina.org/reports/job-growth-in-clean-energy.pdf.

151 "Advisory Panel on Coal Communities," *Alberta Government*, https://www.alberta.ca/coal-communities.aspx.; Ian Bickis, "Alberta communities begin preparing for life after coal," *Global News*, June 22, 2016, http://globalnews.ca/news/2779788/alberta-communities-begin-preparing-for-life-after-coal/.

152 "Carbon levy and rebates," *Alberta Government*, https://www.alberta.ca/climate-carbon-pricing.aspx#p184s4; Jeyakumar, *Job Growth*.

153 Diane Cardwell, "Wind Project in Wyoming Envisions Coal Miners as Trainees," *The New York Times*, May 21, 2017, https://www.nytimes.com/2017/05/21/business/energy-environment/wind-turbine-job-training-wyoming.html?_r=0.

154 Iron & Earth, "Solar Skills," http://www.ironandearth.org/solar_skills.

# SELECT BIBLIOGRAPHY

The following resources were very useful in writing this book, and will help further your understanding of many of the topics the book touches on. You can find more resources in the individual chapter endnotes.

## BOOKS, ARTICLES AND SELECT REPORTS

Aro, Eva-Mari. "From first generation biofuels to advanced solar biofuels." *Ambio* 45, Suppl. 1 (2016): S24–S31. doi:10.1007/s13280-015-0730-0.

BP. BP *Statistical Review of World Energy June 2016* (UK: Pureprint, 2016). https://www.bp.com/content/dam/bp/pdf/energy-economics/statistical-review-2016/bp-statistical-review-of-world-energy-2016-full-report.pdf.

Crone, Patricia. *Pre-Industrial Societies: Anatomy of the Pre-Modern World.* London: Oneworld Publications, 2003. Kindle edition.

Doshi, Amar, Sean Pascoe, Louisa Coglan and Thomas J. Rainey. "Economic and policy issues in the production of algae-based biofuels: A review." *Renewable and Sustainable Energy Reviews* 64 (2016): 329–37. doi:10.1016/j.rser.2016.06.027.

Findlay, Peter. *The Future of the Canadian Oil Sands: Growth potential of a unique resource amidst regulation, egress, cost, and price uncertainty*, OIES Paper: WPM 64 (Oxford: University of Oxford, Oxford Institute for Energy Studies, 2016). https://www.oxfordenergy.org/wpcms/wp-content/uploads/2016/02/The-Future-of-the-Canadian-Oil-Sands-WPM-64.pdf.

Fouquet, Roger, and Peter Pearson. "Past and prospective energy transitions: insights from history." *Energy Policy* 50 (2012): 1–7. doi:10.1016/j.enpol.2012.08.014.

Frank, Richard A., James W. Roy, Greg Bickerton, Steve J. Rowland, John V. Headley, Alan G. Scarlett, Charles E. West et al. "Profiling Oil Sands Mixtures from Industrial Developments and Natural Groundwaters for Source Identification." *Environmental Science & Technology* 48 (2014): 2660–70. doi:10.1021/es500131k.

Frankfurt School-UNEP Centre/BNEF. *Global Trends in Renewable Energy Investment 2016.* http://fs-unepcentre.org/sites/default/files/publications/globaltrendsinrenewableenergyinvestment2016lowres_0.pdf.

Hasler K., S. Bröring, S.W.F. Omta and H.-W. Olfs. "Life cycle assessment (LCA) of different fertilizer product types." *European Journal of Agronomy* 69 (2015): 41–51. doi:10.1016/j.eja.2015.06.001.

Hebert, Craig E., David Campbell, Rhona Kindopp, Stuart MacMillan, Pamela Martin, Ewa Neugebauer, Lucy Patterson et al. "Mercury Trends in Colonial Waterbird Eggs Downstream of the Oil Sands Region of

Alberta, Canada." *Environmental Science and Technology* 47 (2013): 11785–92. doi:10.1021/es402542w.

Hollywood, Emma. "Mining, Migration and Immobility: Towards an understanding of the relationship between migration and occupation in the context of the UK mining industry." *International Journal of Population Geography* 8 (2002): 297–314. doi:10.1002/ijpg.264.

Intergovernmental Panel on Climate Change. *Climate Change 2014 Synthesis Report: Summary for Policymakers* (Geneva, Switzerland: IPCC, 2014). http://www.ipcc.ch/pdf/assessment-report/ar5/syr/AR5_SYR_FINAL_SPM.pdf.

Jacobson, Mark Z., and Cristina L. Archer. "Saturation wind power potential and its implications for wind energy." *PNAS* 109 (2007): 15679–84. doi:10.1073/pnas.1208993109/-/DCSupplemental.

Kelley, Colin P., Shahrzad Mohtadi, Mark A. Cane, Richard Seager and Yochanan Kushnir. "Climate change in the Fertile Crescent and implications of the recent Syrian drought." *PNAS* 112 (2015): 3241–46. doi:10.1073/pnas.1421533112.

Kelly, Erin N., David W. Schindler, Peter V. Hodson, Jeffrey W. Short, Roseanna Radmanovich and Charlene C. Nielsen. "Oil sands development contributes elements toxic at low concentrations to the Athabasca River and its tributaries." *PNAS* 107 (2010): 16178–83. doi:10.1073/pnas.1008754107.

Kelly, Erin N., Jeffrey W. Short, David W. Schindler, Peter V. Hodson, Mingsheng Ma, Alvin K. Kwan and Barbra L. Fortin. "Oil sands development contributes polycyclic aromatic compounds to the Athabasca River and its tributaries." *PNAS* 106 (2009): 22346–51. doi:10.1073/pnas.0912050106.

Kurek, Joshua, Jane L. Kirk, Derek C.G. Muir, Xiaowa Wang, Marlene S. Evans and John P. Smola. "Legacy of a half century of Athabasca oil sands development recorded by lake ecosystems." *PNAS* 110 (2013): 1761–66. doi:10.1073/pnas.1217675110.

Leeson, D., N. Mac Dowell, N. Shah, C. Petit and P.S. Fennell. "A Techno-economic analysis and systematic review of carbon capture and storage (CCS) applied to the iron and steel, cement, oil refining and pulp and paper industries, as well as other high purity sources." *International Journal of Greenhouse Gas Control* 61 (2017): 71–84. doi:10.1016/j.ijggc.2017.03.020.

Malm, Andreas. *Fossil Capital: The Rise of Steam Power and the Roots of Global Warming.* London: Verso, 2016. Kindle edition.

Mikisew Cree First Nation. *Petition to the World Heritage Committee Requesting Inclusion of Wood Buffalo National Park on the List of World Heritage in Danger.* http://cpawsnab.org/uploads/Mikisew_Petition_respecting_UNESCO_Site_256_-_December_8,_2014.PDF.

Mills, Evan. "Job creation and energy savings through a transition to modern off-grid lighting." *Energy for Sustainable Development* 33 (2016): 155–66. doi:10.1016/j.esd.2016.06.001.

Morris, Charles. *Tesla Motors: How Elon Musk and Company Made Electric Cars Cool, and Sparked the Next Tech Revolution.* USA: Bluespages, 2014. Kindle edition.

Pandey, Bhanu, Madhoolika Agrawal and Siddharth Singh. "Assessment of air pollution around coal mining area: Emphasizing on spatial distributions, seasonal variations and heavy metals, using cluster and principal component analysis." *Atmospheric Pollution Research* 5 (2014): 79–86. doi:10.5094/APR.2014.010.

Pandey, Jitendra, Dheeraj Kumar, Virendra Kumar Singh and Niroj Kumar Mohalik. "Environmental and socio-economic impacts of fire in Jharia coalfield, Jharkhand, India: an appraisal." *Current Science* 110 (2016): 1639–50. doi:10.18520/cs/v110/i9/1639-50.

Renewable Energy Policy Network for the 21st Century, *Renewables 2016: Global Status Report* (Paris: REN21 Secretariat, 2016). http://www.ren21 .net/wp-content/uploads/2016/06/GSR_2016_Full_Report_REN21.pdf.

Saini, Varinder, Ravi P. Gupta and Manoj K. Arora. "Environmental impact studies in coalfields in India: A case study from Jharia coal-field." *Renewable and Sustainable Energy Reviews* 53 (2016): 1222–39. doi:10.1016/j.rser.2015.09.072.

Schindler, David W. "Unravelling the complexity of pollution by the oil sands industry." *PNAS* 111 (2014): 3209–10. doi:10.1073/pnas.1400511111.

Seba, Tony. *Clean Disruption of Energy and Transportation.* US: Tony Seba, 2014. Kindle edition.

Smil, Vaclav. *Energy Transitions: Global and National Perspectives*, 2nd ed. Santa Barbara: Praeger, 2017.

———. *Energy Transitions: History, Requirements, Prospects.* Santa Barbara: Praeger, 2010. Kindle edition.

———. *Energy: A Beginner's Guide.* Oxford: Oneworld Publications, 2006.

———. *Enriching the Earth: Fritz Haber, Carl Bosch, and the Transformation of World Food Production.* Cambridge, MA: Massachusetts Institute of Technology, 2001.

Song, Zongyun, Dongxiao Niu and Xinli Xiao. "Focus on the current competitiveness of coal industry in China: Has the depression time gone?" *Resources Policy* 51 (2017): 172–82. doi:10.1016/j.resourpol.2016.11.011.

Stracher, Glenn B., and Tammy P. Taylor. "The Global Catastrophe." In *Coal and Peat Fires: A Global Perspective: Volume 1: Coal—Geology and Combustion*, edited by Glenn B. Stracher, Anupma Prakash and Ellina V. Sokol, 102–13. Amsterdam: Elsevier, 2011.

Timoney, Kevin P. *A study of Water and Sediment Quality as Related to Public Health Issues, Fort Chipewyan, Alberta*, on behalf of the Nunee Health Board Society, Fort Chipewyan, Alberta. https://sites.ualberta.ca/~swfc /images/fc-final-report-revised-dec2007.pdf.

UNESCO World Heritage Centre and International Union for Conservation of Nature. *Reactive Monitoring Mission to Wood Buffalo National Park, Canada 25 September – 4 October 2016: Mission Report, March 2017.* http:// whc.unesco.org/en/documents/156893.

United Nations. *Paris Agreement.* http://unfccc.int/files/essential_background /convention/application/pdf/english_paris_agreement.pdf.

**Sandeep Pai** is an award-winning investigative reporter and researcher. During his journalism career, he has worked for the special investigation teams of several of India's leading English-language newspapers. He has written extensively about the impacts of fossil fuel extraction, renewable energy and rural development. In 2016 he was awarded the Ramnath Goenka Excellence in Journalism Award, India's most prestigious accolade for investigative reporting. Currently Sandeep is pursuing a PhD at the University of British Columbia, specializing in energy transitions. Prior to UBC he completed an Erasmus Mundus Master of Environmental Sciences, Policy and Management, jointly taught at Central European University, Hungary, and Lund University, Sweden. He also holds an engineering degree and postgraduate diploma in journalism, both from India. Sandeep Pai lives in Vancouver, BC.

**Savannah Carr-Wilson** works in the field of environmental and Aboriginal law in British Columbia. Passionate about protecting the global environment, Savannah has worked in environmental law and policy not only in Canada but also internationally with the United Nations Economic Commission for Europe, Secretariat of the Water Convention, and the German non-profit Welthungerhilfe. She has authored several influential reports and publications on environmental topics ranging from the impacts of fossil fuel extraction to the intricacies of water law and policy. She studied law at the University of Victoria, specializing in environmental law and sustainability, and recently completed an Erasmus Mundus Master of Environmental Sciences, Policy and Management, jointly taught at Central European University, Hungary, and Lund University, Sweden. She also holds an undergraduate degree in politics and history from Jacobs University in Bremen, Germany. Savannah Carr-Wilson lives in Vancouver, BC.